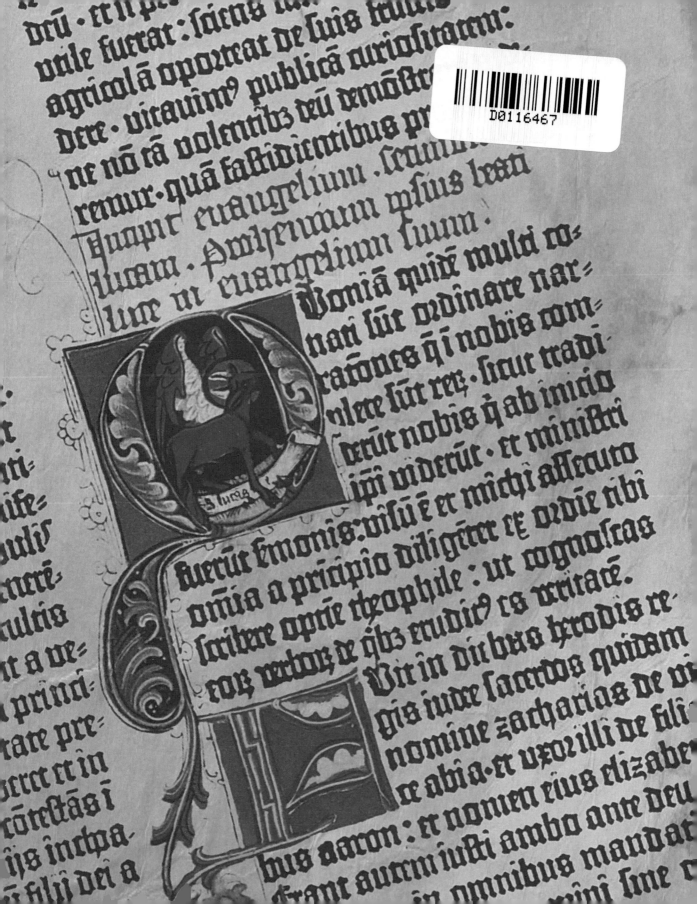

drū · et in pre[...]
vtile fuerat : sciens [...]
agricolā oporteat de suis fructi-
dere · vitauim⁹ publicā curiositatem :
ne nō tā volentibz dꝫu demōstra-
retur · quā fastidientibus pre[...]
Jnatpit euangelium · secundū
lucam · Argumentum ipsius beati
lucē vt euangelium suum .

Quoniā quidē multi co-
nari sūt ordinare nar-
rationes quę ĩ nobis com-
plete sūt rer · sicut tradi-
derūt nobis quĩ ab initio
ipĩ viderūt · et ministri
fuerūt sermonis : visū ē et michi assecuto
omnia a principio diligenter ex ordie tibi
scribere optime theophile : ut cognosce̅
rox verborū de quibus eruditꝰ es veritate̅.
Vir in diebus herodis re-
gis iudee sacerdos quidam
nomine zacharias de vi-
ce abia · et vxor illi de fili-
bus aaron : et nomen eius elizabe[...]
erant autem iusti ambo ante deu[...]
in omnibus mandati[...]
[...]ni sine

THE
BIBLE
COMPANION

First edition published by Parragon in 2013

Parragon
Chartist House
15–17 Trim Street
Bath BA1 1HA, UK
www.parragon.com

Created by Moseley Road Inc.
Editorial Director Lisa Purcell   Art Director Brian MacMullen
Written by Barbara Calamari   Edited by Edward Sczesnak
Designed by Terasa Bernard, Brian MacMullen Production by Holly Lee, Patrick Johnson,
                                                        Danielle Scaramuzzo

ISBN 978-1-78186-621-4

Printed in China

THE
BIBLE
COMPANION

PaRragon

Bath · New York · Singapore · Hong Kong · Cologne · Delhi
Melbourne · Amsterdam · Johannesburg · Shenzhen

TABLE OF CONTENTS

Introduction

The Sacred Book

The Bible—considered the sacred word of God by millions of people worldwide—consists of 66 different books composed by a diverse group of prophets, kings, statesmen, shepherds, poets, tax collectors, musicians, fishermen, and priests. Spanning a period of approximately 1,600 years and written in Hebrew, Aramaic, and Greek, the Bible begins at the dawn of creation and ends with an apocalypse and the Final Judgment. Containing poetry, proverbs, historical narration, laws, and prophecy, many believers of many different faiths rely on the Bible as an invaluable source book for solving practical everyday problems, and they also turn to it for comfort in difficult times.

Our modern-day laws, governments, literature—not to mention our concepts of human rights, morality, and religious worship—are all heavily indebted to the Bible's contents. In the Bible, humankind, though fashioned in God's image, is imperfect and frequently fails. Yet, despite our imperfections, the possibility of redemption—of making ourselves right with God—exists not just as a possibility but as an actual imperative, a crucial goal toward which we all must strive.

The word *bible* is derived from the Koine Greek *ta biblia*, which translates literally as "the books." Referred to as *biblia sacra*, or "sacred book" in medieval Latin, we know it in English today as the Holy Bible. Its writings make up the fundamental religious teachings of Judaism and Christianity, placing it, for followers of Islam, next to the Holy Koran. For Jews, the Bible consists of the 39 books that Christians refer to as the "Old Testament," the most significant being the first five, known as the Pentateuch, which make up the Hebrew Torah. All Christian religions recognize the importance of these 39 books, with Catholic and Orthodox believers including in their versions the seven additional apocryphal books.

Whereas the Old Testament establishes God's relationship and covenant with the Jewish people, the New Testament further expands it, opening it to anyone who is willing to listen and follow. To Christians, these 27 books chronicle the life of the man they believe to be the Messiah, whose coming is predicted in the scripture of the Old Testament: Jesus Christ.

The first scriptures were recorded somewhere around 1000 BCE, but the oldest surviving copies are the Dead Sea Scrolls, which date from 100 BCE. A relatively recent archeological find, these scrolls represent every book of

OPPOSITE PAGE:
The Expulsion from Paradise

The Finding of Moses

the Old Testament with the exception of the Book of Esther. Though the letters from Paul the Apostle and the four Gospels were written in the first century CE, the first complete versions of the New Testament date from the second century CE; the addition of certain epistles and the Book of Revelation to the canon came a century later.

Jews have been using certain books of the Old Testament in religious services for thousands of years, but the division of the Bible into chapter and verse did not occur until the ninth century CE. The modern divisions still employed today were an innovation introduced by a French cardinal, Hugh of Saint-Cher, in the mid-thirteenth century. This arrangement, which greatly enhanced the ability to

reference particular quotes and lessons, was expanded to the New Testament in the mid-sixteenth century. In comparing various versions of the scriptures found in different countries over the preceding two thousand years, it is interesting to note that, though they were passed down through the ages by scribes who were writing by hand, there are, in fact, surprisingly few variations between them. In fact, the 1611 Old Testament version of the King James Bible (the basis of our modern translations) and the 100 BCE Dead Sea Scrolls are almost identical.

BEFORE THERE WERE any written scriptures, the story of the world's creation and the history of the Jewish people had been communicated orally. Moses is credited with writing the first five books of the Bible, after leading his people out of Egypt in 1250 BCE and receiving the law on Mount Sinai—though this idea is disputed by scholars and historians, who believe the first written pieces of the Bible did not appear until 900 BCE.

Genesis, Exodus, Leviticus, Numbers, and Deuteronomy—the first five books—are crucial to Jewish identity and worship tradition. Genesis immediately establishes what was, in ancient times, a unique view of the existence of the one God, as it tells the story of earth's creation, the first humans, and God's covenant and promise to the Jewish people through their forefather, Abraham. In Exodus, we see that covenant in action, as Moses, following divine instruction, leads his people out of slavery and receives the Ten Commandments, as well as religious and cultural laws to follow. By the end of Deuteronomy, a completely new faith, dependent on tribal identity and the obeying of the law, is born.

Much of the Old Testament is devoted to the Historical Books. After Joshua conquers Canaan, establishing the Jewish homeland, we witness the rise and fall of earthly kingdoms, along the way meeting incredible characters and deeply flawed leaders. When the people are faithful, peace and prosperity reign; when they turn their back on God, troubles and disaster run rampant throughout the land.

Poems, prayers, sayings, and stories make up the timeless Wisdom Books.

Men and women of any faith can relate to the universally understandable insights of Psalms, Proverbs, Job, and Ecclesiastes. And the Song of Solomon remains one of the most sensual love poems ever written.

The Old Testament ends with the 17 prophetic books, Isaiah to Malachi. The prophets, considered God's mouthpieces, continually reminded the people to keep their covenant and renew their faith. Unfortunately, the bulk of their warnings went unheeded, and through hubris and poor leadership the nation of Israel was divided and eventually destroyed. With Jerusalem a remnant, the prophets allude to the coming of an ideal king—a holy messiah who will deliver a despondent people and accomplish what no earthly king ever could.

The Prophet Isaiah

The four-hundred-year period between the last Old Testament chapter and the first chapter of the New Testament contains a legacy of near-extinction for the Jews, a successful fight for liberation and sovereignty during the Maccabean period, and, by the first century BCE, a return to living under the control of a foreign empire. Jerusalem is once again a thriving city, and the Temple of Solomon, rebuilt by Herod, is now one of the wonders of the world. Yet there is great dissatisfaction and political division among the various Jewish sects. Anger roils between those who are profiting from their collaboration with their Roman overseers and those who are agitating for rebellion and a return to self-rule. Many religious Jews are waiting for the promised messiah to deliver the nation from servitude.

The Annunciation

Obligingly, the New Testament opens with the Gospel According to Saint Matthew, a description of the birth of Jesus, who is to herald a spectacular change in the way the covenant with God is interpreted. Rejected by Jews and embraced by Christians as "the good news" that Jesus is, indeed, the Messiah foretold by the Old Testament prophets, the 27 New Testament books begin with the four Gospels detailing Jesus's life and religious mission, two of which are written by his disciples Matthew and John. The Gospel According to Saint Mark, allegedly dictated by the leader of the apostles, Peter, while he was in prison in Rome, is the oldest and briefest, while the Gospel According to Saint Luke, written by a follower of Paul, is a result of its author's wide-ranging research, an accumulation of written texts and interviews with living witnesses to Jesus's life. Luke is also credited with writing the Acts of the Apostles, which details Christ's ascension into Heaven and the descent of the Holy Spirit upon His followers.

When Peter has his revelation—that Jesus welcomes all to believe in him, not just Jews—Paul, once the greatest persecutor of Christians, a hater of non-Jews, becomes the Apostle to the Gentiles. Paul's 13 letters to members of the early church grant us a real-time view of the problems, scriptural misinterpretations, and persecution faced by early Christians. There are also letters from Peter, James, John, and Jude on matters of

faith and encouragement. The New Testament closes with the mysterious and visually rich Book of Revelation, as otherworldly as the Epistles can be practical and down-to-earth, detailing John's visions of the end of the world and the coming Day of Judgment.

Enormously influential, closely studied, widely quoted, the Bible remains one of the most astonishing literary efforts humanity has ever produced—"the greatest story ever lived" by the thousands—including Jesus—who suffered the ignominies of biblical times, as recorded by the hundreds who chronicled their many sins and sacrifices along the arduous path to a more perfect realization of faith.

Jesus Christ rules from on high through the words of the Bible.

Noah's Ark

THE OLD TESTAMENT

THE ANCIENT NEAR EAST

Within the "Fertile Crescent" that stretched from the Tigris and Euphrates Rivers west to the coast of the Mediterranean and south to the Nile Valley, arose the world's oldest civilizations. These places form the backdrop for the stories of the Old Testament.

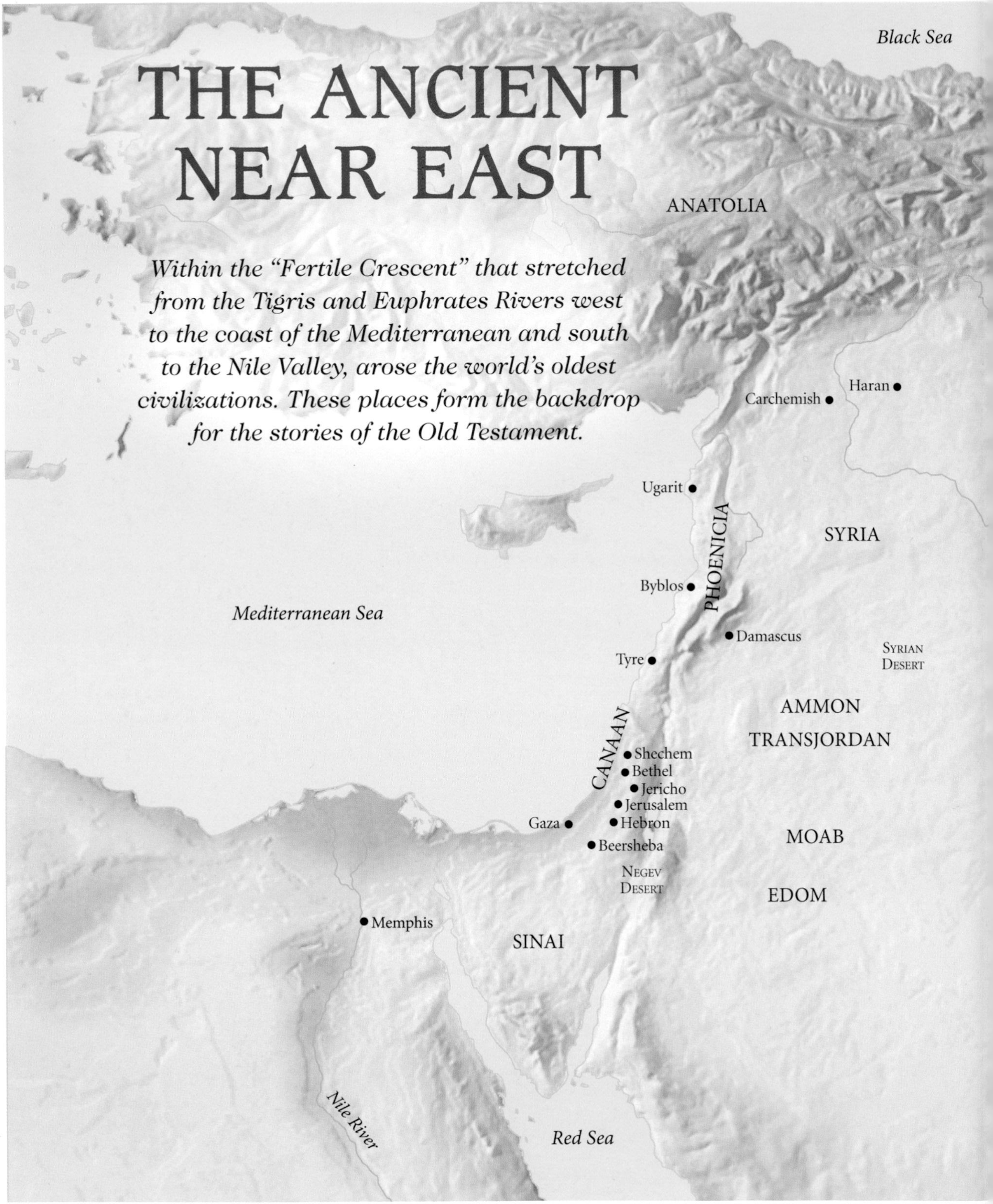

Black Sea

ANATOLIA

Carchemish •

Haran •

Ugarit •

PHOENICIA

SYRIA

Mediterranean Sea

Byblos •

• Damascus

SYRIAN DESERT

Tyre •

CANAAN

AMMON

TRANSJORDAN

• Shechem
• Bethel
• Jericho
• Jerusalem

Gaza • • Hebron

• Beersheba

MOAB

NEGEV DESERT

EDOM

• Memphis

SINAI

Nile River

Red Sea

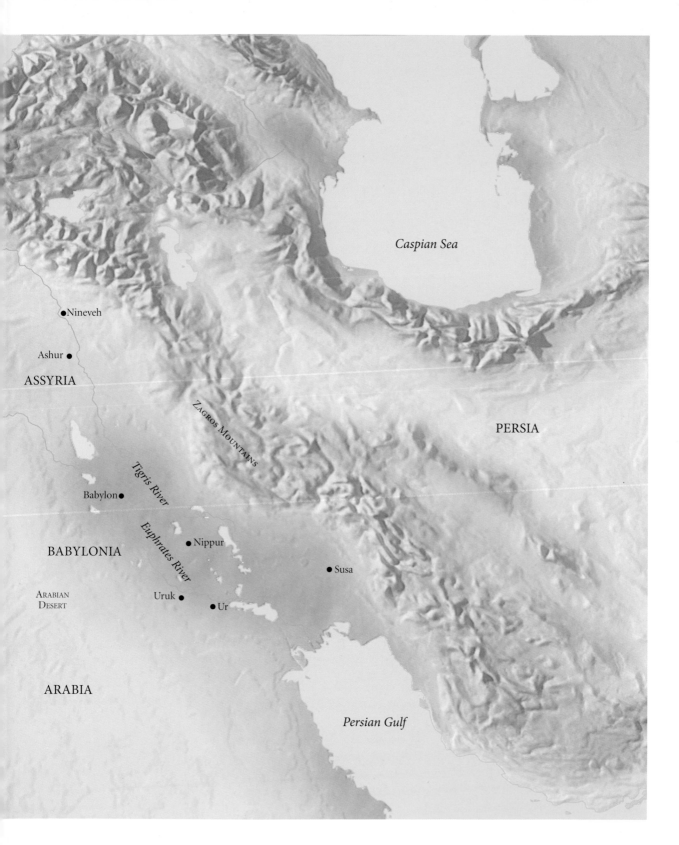

Caspian Sea

● Nineveh

Ashur ●

ASSYRIA

ZAGROS MOUNTAINS

PERSIA

Tigris River

Babylon ●

Euphrates River

BABYLONIA

● Nippur

ARABIAN
DESERT

Uruk ●

● Susa

● Ur

ARABIA

Persian Gulf

The
Pentateuch

The term "Old Testament" refers to the Hebrew books of the Bible that recount the history of the Jewish people prior to the coming of Jesus Christ. Its first five books—Genesis, Exodus, Leviticus, Numbers, and Deuteronomy—appear in both the Christian and Hebrew Bibles. Jewish tradition refers to these books as the Torah, meaning "the law"; Christian tradition names them the Pentateuch, from the Greek for "five-volumed." Though many religions disagree about the books and translations that make up the entire Old Testament, all include these five books and the later books of the Hebrew prophets, scriptures, and psalms.

Various authors wrote the Old Testament over a period of hundreds of years, beginning in the fifth century BCE. It establishes the existence of a monotheistic, world-creating God and his special covenant with the people of Israel. The Pentateuch is the most significant section, in which God hands down His basic laws to Moses. The basis of our modern laws is set down here, with its insistence on morality, judicial fairness, obedience, and faithfulness. The remainder, written much later, narrates the history of the Jewish people, emphasizing the eternal battle between good and evil as well as the consequences of turning one's back on God.

Adam and Eve in the Garden of Eden

THE BOOK OF
GENESIS

GOD IS THE MOST PROMINENT FORCE IN THE FIRST
BOOK OF THE BIBLE, WHICH CHRONICLES THE
DAWN OF ALL CREATION.

The word *genesis* means "origin," and the Book of Genesis describes the origins of the universe—how the one and only God forms it and how all was darkness until He creates light. The hand of God forms the earth and all living creatures, ferocious and gentle.

This book also explains the origins of the first humans, Adam and Eve. Along with their expulsion from the Garden of Eden, Genesis shows how their sinful acts underlie the suffering that plagues humankind to this day.

Apart from recounting the history of Adam and Eve's early descendants, Genesis also tells of God's disgust with the wickedness of humanity and of His desire to wipe out what He has created in order to start over. Finding a righteous man named Noah, He orders him to build an ark and take his family onboard, along with two of every

Earthly Paradise for Adam and Eve

creature. As soon as Noah completes this task, God unleashes upon the world the Great Flood, lasting forty days and forty nights. When the torrent

> In the beginning God created the heaven and the earth.
>
> GENESIS 1:1

is over, it is up to Noah and his family to repopulate the planet; Noah's sons spread to every corner of the world, inhabiting every nation.

Genesis also details the harsh judgments God metes out in the collapse of the Tower of Babel and the destruction of Sodom and Gomorrah. Ever ready to punish the wicked, God also makes a covenant with Abraham after he withstands a severe test of faith. God shows Abraham Canaan, future home of the Israelites, and promises it to his people in exchange for keeping their agreement with the Lord. Genesis also foretells that before they settle in the Promised Land, God's people will endure much hardship, as well as hundreds of years in a foreign country. Jacob, grandson of Abraham, fathers a dozen sons, subsequently known as the patriarchs of the Twelve Tribes of Israel. The book follows Joseph, one of Jacob's sons, through a series of remarkable travails. When Joseph triumphantly reemerges with an important position in Egypt, the tribes follow him there to avoid the catastrophic famine overtaking their land. Genesis ends with the Hebrew nation settling in Egypt.

Creation

IN THE BEGINNING OF GENESIS, GOD CREATES
THE UNIVERSE, INCLUDING ALL THE ELEMENTS,
ALL THE ANIMALS, AND, FINALLY, HUMANKIND.

The very first words of the Bible, "In the beginning God created the heaven and the earth. And the earth was without form and void . . ." establish God as the sole creator and ruling power over all nature and every living creature. Creation begins with God forming the universe (a task completed in six days) and continues on to detail the formation of all the elements and creatures of the earth. Man, God's final and most exalted creation, made in his image, receives the earth to cultivate and accepts dominance over all other creatures. Creation ends on the seventh day when God, happy with all he has achieved, rests and blesses the day as holy. He commands humankind to keep it special and set it apart from the other days of the week.

The Creation of Fishes and Birds

The Creation of Adam

The Creation of the Animals

THE SEVEN DAYS OF CREATION

Day One: All is darkness and formless. God creates light, which He separates from darkness. He establishes *day* and *night*.

Day Two: God creates the sky.

Day Three: God separates the waters from the dry land, establishing land and sea. He also creates plants and trees.

Day Four: God creates the stars, sun, and moon, in order to separate day from night and to mark the passage of the seasons.

Day Five: God fills the skies and the seas with life by creating birds and fishes. Pleased with these new life-forms, He commands them to increase and multiply.

Day Six: To fill the earth, God creates every kind of animal, domesticated and wild. As His final act of creation, God forms human beings in His own image. He blesses them, telling them to "be fruitful and multiply" so that their descendants will inhabit the entire earth. He grants humans dominion over nature and animals and tells them to care for and cultivate the earth.

Day Seven: Happy with all that He has created, God stops working and rests. He sanctifies the seventh day as sacred and orders humankind to keep it separate from the other six days of the week.

The first part of Creation depicts the world as God intended it to be, with all creatures and life-forms coexisting and providing for one another. In this idyllic paradise, God expresses contentment and satisfaction with all that He surveys.

Adam and Eve

THE SECOND PART OF GENESIS
TELLS THE STORY OF ADAM AND EVE,
THE MOTHER AND FATHER OF THE HUMAN RACE.

It is not long after Adam and Eve's creation that with their actions they introduce disobedience, sin, judgment, guilt, and shame into the world.

Taking soil from the ground, God forms Adam, breathing life into him. God places him in a lush and beautiful garden created especially for him. Adam is free to eat and do whatever he likes, with one stipulation: "You may eat the fruit of any tree in the garden," God tells him, "except the tree that gives knowledge of what is good and what is bad." If Adam eats from that tree, he will die the same day.

After creating all the birds and animals, God then decides that Adam needs a more suitable companion. God puts him in a deep sleep and then, using one of Adam's own ribs, forms Eve. Though naked, the pair live happily together, without any sense of shame.

One day, a snake asks Eve why neither she nor Adam have ever eaten from the tree of knowledge. She answers that if they do, they will die. The snake then tells her that if they eat the fruit they will possess the same knowledge as God. Thinking about how wonderful it would be to be wise, Eve bites into the fruit and then offers some to

her husband. As soon as they swallow it, they realize that they are naked. Later that evening, when God asks them why they are hiding from him, Adam tells

Adam and Eve

> And Adam called his wife's name Eve; because she was the mother of all living.
>
> GENESIS 3:20

God that he is ashamed of his nakedness. When God asks if it is true that they had eaten the forbidden fruit, Adam blames Eve; she, in turn, blames the snake for tricking her into disobeying God.

As punishment, rather than a death sentence, God condemns snakes to crawl on their bellies forever and to be enemies of the human race. He orders Eve to have great pains in childbirth and Adam to toil on the earth to obtain food. God gives them animal skins to wear and banishes them from the Garden of Eden to live out in the world and cultivate the soil from which they were created.

The Haywain Triptych

Expulsion from the Garden of Eden

Noah and the Flood

GOD BRINGS FORTH A WORLDWIDE DELUGE
TO CLEANSE THE EARTH, BUT HE SAVES NOAH
BECAUSE HE LIVES A RIGHTEOUS LIFE.

As the descendants of Adam and Eve spread throughout the world, the evil deeds and violent acts of humankind greatly disturb God. He therefore decides to destroy every living creature on earth in order to cleanse it. God makes an exception, though, and decides to spare Noah, who lives a righteous life. God instructs Noah to build a boat large enough to carry his wife, his three sons and their wives, and a pair of every animal species on earth. Noah does everything that God commands.

Seven days before the flood begins, Noah and his family load the ark. Exactly as God said it would, a torrential rain begins to pelt the earth. Noah and his family board the ark. The rain continues for forty days and forty nights, so saturating the earth that even the great mountain ranges lie twenty-five feet underwater. The catastrophic flood destroys all living creatures on earth—the only things still alive are the animals on Noah's Ark.

As the ark travels through the floodwaters, God commands a wind to blow, causing the waters to recede. When the rain stops, Noah opens a window and sends out a raven. When the raven fails to return with evidence of dry land, Noah sends out a dove, which returns because it finds no place to land. Noah waits another seven days before sending it out again. This time the dove comes back with an olive branch in its beak, a sign that the waters are quickly receding.

Noah's Ark

Building the Ark

> There went in two and two unto Noah
> into the ark, the male and the female,
> as God had commanded Noah.
>
> GENESIS 7:9

Noah and his family leave the ark when the water is gone, unloading all the animals and birds. God then makes a covenant with Noah, promising never again to destroy every living creature. Blessing Noah and his family, God exhorts them to have many children in order to repopulate the earth. He also places under their power all plants and animals to use as food. His only demand is that they not eat any animal with blood still in it, as blood contains life. And as a symbol of his pledge not to wipe out life on earth again, God places a rainbow in the sky, signifying the promise he has made to all his creatures.

The Dove returns to Noah

The Subsiding of the waters of the Deluge

BIRDS OF THE BIBLE

The Old and New Testaments contain hundreds of references to birds. Along with using birds as metaphors, the Bible's scribes were obviously birdwatchers, tracking the behavior and habits of many avian species. This is just a sampling.

ALONG WITH THE classification of land and sea creatures, the Bible also speaks of "clean" and "unclean" birds. Clean birds, including the dove, turtledove, quail, sparrow, swallow, pigeon, partridge, crane, rooster, and

The Apostle Peter denies Jesus three times before the rooster crows.

hen, may be eaten or used in a sacrifice to God. Unclean birds are considered an abomination to eat or sacrifice. They include the eagle, ossifrage, osprey, vulture, raven, owl, hawk,

All four Gospels liken the spirit of God to a dove. A dove descends above Jesus after His baptism (Matthew 3:1; Matthew 16:1; Mark 1:10; Luke 3:22; John 1:32)

cuckoo, cormorant, swan, pelican, stork, heron, lapwing, ostrich, and peacock.

Biblical scribes utilized much of what they learned about birds to form metaphors in their writing. Birds as symbols

The eagle has a prominent role in the Bible.

appear throughout the Bible. The eagle, honored for its swiftness and strength, often stands for divine watchfulness, and artists frequently choose an eagle to symbolize John

> Like a crane *or* a swallow, so did I chatter:
> I did mourn as a dove: mine eyes fail *with looking* upward.
>
> ISAIAH 38:14

The swallow is thought of as a clean bird and is mentioned many times in the Bible.

the Evangelist. Passages in which the eagle represents evil may be mistranslations; the original writer most likely had a vulture in mind. This "unclean" scavenger brought forth fears of a dreadful fate—that of dying and being left unburied to become vulture food.

All four Gospel writers use a dove to represent the spirit of God. In the Old Testament, Noah

The "lowly" sparrow is important in a key passage of Jesus's teachings.

knows it is safe to disembark when the dove comes back carrying an olive branch. The dove also signifies rejoicing after a long period of darkness.

Because it feeds Elijah in the desert, the raven, a common scavenger bird in Israel, symbolizes the hermit. In the Bible, the name *sparrow* denotes several different species of birds, all of which eat grain and insects and gather in noisy flocks. These little birds are such social creatures that a solitary sparrow is considered a symbol of deep loneliness (Psalm 102:7). People consider sparrows so insignificant that, with the purchase of three, sellers would include an extra one for free. It is the always-compassionate Jesus who, referring to this extra sparrow, said ". . . and not one of them is forgotten before God" (Luke 12:4–7). God takes note of even the littlest among us.

The rooster is also a familiar symbol of the Christian Passion. Prior to his arrest by Roman soldiers, Jesus correctly predicts that Peter will deny him three times before the rooster crows the following morning.

The raven was used to symbolize evil and unrest.

The Ancestors

THE BIBLE TELLS US THAT THE WHOLE HUMAN RACE DESCENDS FROM NOAH AND HIS THREE SONS, SHEM, HAM, AND JAPHETH.

According to the Bible, we are all descendants of Noah. His three sons—Shem, Ham, and Japheth—are each associated with different peoples and regions of the world. The Bible lists seventy nations that trace their origins to the sons of Noah.

Biblical scholars say that the descendants of Japheth, the oldest, migrated to what is now Europe and India. Many believe the Caucasian peoples, or Indo-Europeans, came through Japheth's lineage.

Noah's sons—(L–R) Shem, Ham, and Japheth

> These are the families of the sons of Noah, after their generations, in their nations: and by these were the nations divided in the earth after the flood.
>
> GENESIS 10:32

Ham is thought to be the forefather of the African peoples, including the Egyptians, as well as Arabians and Babylonians. Ham's descendants populated Asia, so he is also considered the progenitor of the Asiatic peoples. The offspring of Shem, Noah's second son, did not migrate to other lands, as his brothers' children did. He is the forefather of the Semitic peoples who now populate the Middle East. Both Arabs and Jews claim Shem as their ancestor.

Because the Hebrews are said to have descended from Shem, it is his lineage that the Bible follows.

Many generations after Shem, his descendant Terah takes his son, Abram; his son's wife, Sarai; and his grandson, Lot; and they leave their home in Babylon to settle in Haran. It is Abram with whom God will make his next covenant.

BABYLONIA

PRIOR TO THE MOVEMENT of Noah's sons, the world's population, united by a single language, had settled in Babylonia. There, members of all three tribes decide that they will together build a magnificent city with a tower that reaches the sky. When God sees this, however, He disapproves of their hubris. Realizing that a common language makes cooperation among tribes too easy, God decides to mix up language; no longer will those of different tribes understand one another. Unable to communicate, the builders stop working on the tower and scatter to their own tribes, eventually moving farther and farther away—a relatively simple matter in these times, as the earth is a single land mass. The descendants of Japheth move to the north and west, the descendants of Ham move to the south, and the descendants of Shem stay in the same place. According to the Bible, it is during the time of Peleg, one of Shem's descendants, that the earth splits into continents, thus further dividing the original tribes from one another and eventually resulting in the development of many different cultures and languages.

Babylon Fallen

Tower of Babel

Life of Abraham

GOD GIVES ABRAHAM A SON, ISAAC, AND THEN TESTS
ABRAHAM. GOD ASKS ABRAHAM TO SACRIFICE HIS SON,
WHO WAS MOST PRECIOUS TO HIM.

Considered the father of both the Arab and Jewish peoples, Abraham, born in Babylonia as from battles with neighboring kings and witnesses the destruction of the wicked Sodom and Gomorrah.

> And Isaac spake unto Abraham his father, and said, My father: and he said, Here am I, my son. And he said, Behold the fire and the wood: but where is the lamb for a burnt offering?
>
> GENESIS 22:7

Hagar in the Wilderness

Abram, experiences remarkable events in his 175 years. He sees the rescue of his nephew Lot

When Abram is 75 years old, God tells him to uproot his household and move to the

land of Canaan. Driven out by a famine, Abram, his wife, Sarai, and Lot move to Egypt. Expelled from that country, they decide that Lot should settle on the outskirts of Sodom, while Abram and Sarai should stay in Hebron, part of Canaan.

God comes to Abram in a deep sleep, telling him that his descendants will be enslaved for four hundred years. Only then will they return to Canaan and receive all the land there.

Because Sarai is barren, she suggests that Abram father a child with Hagar, her slave. Hagar duly bears him a son, who they call Ishmael. Abram is now 86 years old.

Abraham Journeying into the land of Canaan

Thirteen years later, God again appears to Abram—this time to make a formal covenant. He promises Abram many descendants, who will inherit the entire nation of Canaan. He changes Abram's name to Abraham, meaning "father of many nations." God also commands that Abraham and all the males of his household undergo circumcision, an outward sign of this everlasting covenant. Changing Sarai's name to Sarah, God tells her that she will give birth to Abraham's son. Abraham and Sarah find themselves, at the respective ages of 99 and 90, the parents of Isaac.

Eventually, Sarah demands that Abraham send away Hagar and Ishmael, so that Isaac will become Abraham's sole heir. As Ishmael's father, Abraham dislikes this plan, so by way of reassurance, God promises him that Ishmael will found a great nation in his own right.

Abraham's greatest test of faith comes when Isaac is a boy. God orders Abraham to sacrifice the thing in life he cherishes most—his son. Yet, Abraham does not question God's command. As he is about to kill Isaac, an angel stops him, telling him to substitute a wandering ram instead. Pleased by this act of supreme faith, God repeats His promise to Abraham's descendants, and Isaac lives on to continue his bloodline.

The sacrifice of Isaac

Lives of Isaac and Jacob

ISAAC FATHERS TWO SONS, ESAU AND JACOB.
JACOB, THE YOUNGER, FATHERS A DOZEN SONS,
WHO BECOME THE ISRAELITES.

The Bible considers Abraham, Isaac, and Jacob the Patriarchs of Israel. Of the three, Isaac lived the longest and enjoyed the most stable and harmonious life.

To find a wife for Isaac, Abraham sends his most trusted servant from Canaan to his people in Mesopotamia; the servant finds Rebecca there and brings her back. Isaac falls in love instantly and happily marries her.

After two decades of marriage, when Isaac is 60 years old, Rebecca becomes pregnant with twins who, much to her shock, seem to be fighting in her belly. When she asks God what is happening, He tells her that her descendants will become two

Esau Sells his Birthright

rival peoples. Those who descend from her older child will serve the descendants of the younger.

The elder of the twins, Esau, is born red-skinned and hairy. The younger twin, Jacob, comes out of the womb holding his brother's heel. As young men, Esau, his father's favorite, enjoys hunting; Jacob, more refined and spiritual, earns his mother's preference.

One day, Esau returns home extremely hungry and demands that his brother serve him food. Jacob agrees to do it in exchange for Esau's rights as firstborn son. Seeing little value in these privileges, Esau cedes his birthright to Jacob in exchange for a bowl of stew.

Landscape with the marriage of Isaac and Rebecca

Meeting of Jacob and Esau

A birthright is not the only thing Jacob usurps from Esau. When Isaac, blind and old, sends for his firstborn son to give him a blessing, Jacob, disguising himself with Rebecca's help, receives the blessing in his brother's stead. When Esau finds out, he is so enraged that Rebecca has to send Jacob to her homeland to protect him.

Upon reaching his Uncle Laban's house, Jacob falls in love with the youngest daughter, Rachel. For seven years, he works to earn her hand in marriage, only to have Laban substitute his elder daughter, Leah, on the wedding night (the older daughter customarily marries first). Jacob then works another seven years to take Rachel as wife.

Eventually, Jacob returned to Canaan with a daughter and 11 sons. After spending a night wrestling with an angel, he reconciles with his brother, Esau. For showing such fortitude, the angel renames Jacob "Israel."

Rachel dies giving birth to Jacob's twelfth son; each son eventually goes on to found one of the Twelve Tribes of Israel.

Jacob wrestling the Angel

The Life of Joseph

JOSEPH IS ONE OF JACOB'S TWELVE SONS. AFTER HIS BROTHERS
SELL HIM INTO SLAVERY, JOSEPH GOES TO EGYPT, WHERE
HE EVENTUALLY BECOMES A FAVORITE OF THE KING.

Joseph is Jacob's favorite of all of his twelve sons. Living in Canaan, where they work as shepherds, his brothers resent the fact that Joseph often reports their misdeeds to their father. And when he tells them of his dream—that their sheaves of wheat bow down to his—they decide to do away with him. One day, they take away his many-colored coat when Joseph is at work in the pasture, and they sell him into slavery to traders on their way to Egypt. Dousing his coat with goat's blood, they bring it to their father, who surmises that Joseph has been killed by wild animals. Jacob is inconsolable over the loss of his favorite son.

> And Joseph dreamed a dream,
> and he told it his brethren: and
> they hated him yet the more.
>
> GENESIS 37:5

Sold to one of the king's officers, Joseph becomes an indispensable member of

The story of Joseph

the household, yet when he refuses the advances of the officer's wife, she accuses him of molesting her, and he is imprisoned.

Joseph correctly divines the meaning of the dreams of two of the king's servants, who were imprisoned with him. Years later, when the king himself has a troubling dream, the surviving servant tells him about Joseph's talent, and the king brings Joseph before him. Joseph tells the king that his dream means that Egypt will enjoy seven years of plenty, followed by seven years of famine. If the people make great storages of grain in the years of plenty, the nation will survive. The king is so grateful to Joseph that he makes him governor of all Egypt.

The famine that comes is widespread, as Joseph had predicted, and Canaan is hit especially hard. And because Egypt is the only country in the region to have any grain, Jacob sends his sons there to buy some. They bow down to Joseph in honor, not recognizing him,

Jacob and Joseph's Coat

grateful to be able to feed their starving people. When he reveals to them that he is their brother, Joseph, instead of administering the punishment they fear, instructs them to bring all of their people, including Jacob, to live in Egypt, where they

prosper for many years. When Jacob dies, his body is interred in Abraham's tomb. At the end of his life, Joseph, having predicted that his people would one day return to Canaan, requests that his body, too, be buried with those of his forefathers.

Joseph revealing himself to his Brothers

THE BOOK OF
EXODUS

IN THIS BOOK, THE ISRAELITES LEAVE EGYPT AFTER
HUNDREDS OF YEARS OF ENSLAVEMENT. MOSES LEADS
THEM ACROSS THE RED SEA TO MOUNT SINAI.

The word *exodus* comes from the Greek, meaning "departure." In the Book of Exodus, the people of Israel leave behind all that is familiar and learn to live a new life conforming to the Laws of God. Not only does the second book of the Bible detail the liberation of the Israelites from slavery and their departure from Egypt, it also describes the first Passover and reestablishes God's covenant with His people. As the prophet who receives God's guidance and carries out his wishes, Moses is the driving force of Exodus.

Sinking of the Pharaoh in the Red Sea

THE FIRST TABERNACLE

WHILE AT MOUNT SINAI, Moses receives the Ten Commandments, engraved in a stone tablet. In keeping with the covenant between God and his people, God orders the Israelites to follow these moral and religious laws. When he learns that they are worshipping a golden calf, he severely castigates them and issues a very strict and detailed code that includes rules of dress, building materials, priestly duties, and rituals. The code lays the foundation for the construction of the first tabernacle, and in these rules and regulations we find the beginnings of organized Jewish worship.

Moses and the Ten Commandments

Hundreds of years after the death of Joseph, the descendants of the Twelve Tribes of Israel were so numerous that they could be found in every corner of Egypt. As Exodus opens, the Egyptians, God appears as a burning bush, Egypt is afflicted with ten ruinous plagues, the Red Sea parts, and, in the most astounding miracle of all, after 430 years in captivity, every single

> And they made their lives bitter with hard bondage,
> in mortar, and in brick, and in all manner of service
> in the field: all their service, wherein they
> made them serve, was with rigor.
>
> EXODUS 1:14

who fear rebellion and the overthrow of the kingdom, enslave the Israelites, who are then brutally suppressed for hundreds of years. In Exodus, the Pharaoh orders the death of all newborn male Israelites. The story of one of these babies, Moses—who God eventually chooses to be the liberator of the Israelites—is central to the Book of Exodus. Miracles abound: Israelite—more than 600,000 strong— escapes from Egypt to set up camp at Mount Sinai.

Exodus ends as a cloud appears over the Tabernacle, covering the sacred tent erected for worship. The Israelites follow the movements of the cloud, a symbol of God's manifest presence, and He guides His people in their travels through the desert.

The Story of Moses

MOSES IS BORN IN EGYPT, TAKEN IN BY A PRINCESS, AND RAISED AS A PRINCE. WHEN HE BECOMES AN ADULT, GOD SPEAKS TO MOSES AND TELLS HIM TO LEAD HIS PEOPLE OUT OF BONDAGE IN EGYPT.

The story of the life of Moses spans the last four books of the Pentateuch. Moses's lifetime coincides with a pivotal period in the creation of the Jewish religion.

God chooses Moses to lead his people, and Moses fearlessly confronts the pharaoh who has enslaved them, unleashing the Ten Plagues on Egypt. It is Moses who sits with God and receives his law in the form of the Ten Commandments, guiding his people for forty years through the wilderness.

> And the child grew, and she brought him unto Pharaoh's daughter, and he became her son. And she called his name Moses: and she said, Because I drew him out of the water.
>
> EXODUS 2:10

A descendant of the tribe of Levi, Moses is born in Egypt just as the pharaoh orders the slaying of all newborn male Israelites. His mother, placing him in a basket, sends him down the Nile River, where an Egyptian princess finds him and raises him as a prince. As a young man, Moses witnesses an overseer beat a Hebrew slave. Outraged by the injustice, he kills the overseer and flees to Midian to avoid the pharaoh's wrath. There he marries and works as a shepherd. He encounters a burning bush while out in the wilderness; it speaks, ordering him back to Egypt to free his people. God works many miracles through Moses as he accomplishes the deliverance of the Israelites from Egypt.

While camping at Mount Sinai, God invites Moses onto the mountain and gives him the Ten Commandments on two stone tablets. The people come to recognize Moses as the Lawgiver, for it is through him that God communicates all of

Pharaoh's daughter finds Moses in the Nile

Passage of the Jews through the Red Sea

the rules of daily life that He expects His people to observe.

Like God, Moses is constantly disappointed by the Israelites; they complain incessantly, seem to have little faith, and repeatedly break God's law. Yet, when God is angry, Moses frequently intervenes on their behalf. Though God leads them to the Promised Land, the Israelites are too fearful to take possession of it; as punishment, God condemns them to wander the desert for another forty years. Because Moses himself disobeyed God on one occasion, God declares Moses must once again lead his people to the Promised Land, but not enter it himself. Moses dies, having dictated the Laws of God, blessing his people, and looking over the land that was promised to Abraham, Jacob, and Isaac.

Landscape with Moses and the Burning Bush

The Ten Commandments

AFTER MOSES LEADS THE ISRAELITES OUT OF EGYPT,
GOD SUMMONS HIM TO MOUNT SINAI. THERE, GOD
GIVES HIM TWO STONE TABLETS.

Upon their deliverance from Egypt, the children of Israel make camp at the foot of Mount Sinai. There, they set up twelve altars (one for each of the Twelve Tribes of Israel), and the people make sacrifices in celebration of their newfound freedom. God summons Moses to the top of the mountain, where he stays for forty days and forty nights as God dictates new rules for His people to live by.

Unfortunately, the people have no idea why Moses has vanished. Left below, without guidance, they demand that Moses's brother Aaron create some novel way for them to

> And the Lord said unto Moses, Come up to me into the mount, and be there: and I will give thee tables of stone, and a law, and Commandments which I have written; that thou mayest teach them.
>
> EXODUS 24:12

worship God. Aaron has an idea and tells the people to bring their gold and jewels, which he melts down, fashioning a golden calf for them to venerate. Witnessing this display, God, who has given Moses two stone tablets with his sacred commandments etched on them, grows angry, ordering

The Ten Commandments

Moses off the mountain. A puzzled Moses descends Mount Sinai, only to find his people singing and dancing around the golden calf. Furious, Moses hurls God's tablets to the ground, breaking them into pieces.

Death and disease await all who insisted on worshiping the golden idol, but after Moses begs God's forgiveness for the others, God orders him to cut another set of tablets and return to Mount Sinai. Moses stays another forty days and forty nights, and again God chisels the Ten Commandments into stone.

Moses with the Ten Commandments

THE TEN COMMANDMENTS

TODAY, WE FIND the very basis of the laws of Western civilization in the Ten Commandments. Unlike many of the other rules and laws that God gives Moses, these are the fundamental, most important laws God expects his people to live by.

1. I am the Lord thy God . . . Thou shalt have no other gods before me.

2. Thou shalt not make unto thee any graven image.

3. Thou shalt not take the name of the Lord thy God in vain.

4. Remember the sabbath day, to keep it holy.

5. Honor thy father and thy mother.

6. Thou shalt not kill.

7. Thou shalt not commit adultery.

8. Thou shalt not steal.

9. Thou shalt not bear false witness against thy neighbor.

10. Thou shalt not covet thy neighbor's house, thou shalt not covet thy neighbor's wife . . . nor any thing that is thy neighbor's.

The Covenant

IN GENESIS, GOD FIRST ESTABLISHES THE COVENANT THAT HE MAKES WITH HIS PEOPLE. IN EXODUS, GOD REMEMBERS HIS PROMISE AND ASKS THAT THE ISRAELITES HONOR HIM IN RETURN.

The Old Testament tells of many covenants, or solemn agreements, between God and his people. In Genesis, for example, God promises Noah to never again destroy life on earth, sending a rainbow down from the heavens as a symbol of this covenant. He later promises Abraham innumerable descendants, who will always have a special relationship with God and one day inherit the land of Canaan. Circumcision comes to represent this covenant.

Neither of these agreements demands anything from the human race. Not until the Book of Exodus does God expect humankind to honor its obligation by obeying Him and following a very strict set of rituals and laws.

Exodus opens with God recalling His covenant with Abraham, Isaac, and Jacob to watch over their people. Using Moses as His prophet, He frees the Twelve Tribes of Israel from their slavery in Egypt. The Ten Commandments, which Moses receives directly from God three months later, function as a basic contract of behavior between God and humankind.

These laws are divine instructions, so God considers any breach or violation of them a sin, and many of the commandments include specific punishments for breaking them. Obeying God's laws is considered crucial to keeping the covenant alive; in exchange for the faith and respect shown to Him, God promises to watch over the Israelites, giving them special protection. Though they are homeless and wandering in the desert, for example, God promises to give them Canaan as a homeland.

For the first time, the Israelites establish a Jewish identity through prescribed religious rituals and the proper training of priests. God gives Moses highly detailed regulations for building a house of worship, stressing festivals, dietary and cultural rules, and the importance of not intermarrying outside the Twelve Tribes of Israel. The prospect of enduring the wrath of God for violating the agreement becomes a very real possibility. But God's promise to stay and guide His chosen people is just as real.

> And Moses took the blood, and sprinkled it on the people, and said, Behold the blood of the covenant, which the Lord hath made with you concerning all these words.
>
> EXODUS 24:8

Moses destroying the Tablets of the Law

THE BOOK OF
LEVITICUS

THE BOOK OF LEVITICUS CODIFIES GOD'S EXPECTATIONS OF HIS CHOSEN PEOPLE FOR THE FIRST TIME. MANY OF MODERN JUDAISM'S MOST FUNDAMENTAL TENETS TRACE THEIR ROOTS TO THIS TEXT.

God granted Moses the responsibility of organizing the massive exodus of the children of Israel. Coming from a foreign land, where they had lived in disparate communities for more than four hundred years, the people then desired a set of communal laws. After the conflicts of Genesis and Exodus, Leviticus (thus named because only men of the tribe of Levi could enter the priestly caste) offers a sober, somewhat technical series of regulations pertaining to religious worship and daily life for the newly established society of Jewish people.

For example, in ancient times every religion contained some ritual of animal sacrifice. Leviticus differentiates

The feast in the House of Levi

between "clean" and "unclean" animals and gives strict orders for the performance of these sacrificial rituals. Indeed, God destroys Moses's nephews, Nadab and Abihu, when they offer incense in an unholy way.

life. God tells His people how He wants them to be; His rules and regulations distinguish the Tribes of Israel from their neighbors. Yet the most well-known words of this book are God's admonishment to His people to "love

---

And the Lord called unto Moses, and spake unto him
out of the Tabernacle of the Congregation.

LEVITICUS 1:1

Along with rules for priests, Leviticus contains detailed ordinances instructing Israelites in every aspect of daily life: regulations governing diet, hair, money, property, treatment of dead bodies, the consumption of alcohol, skin disease, bodily purification, sexual relations, and the proper definition of "family." God expects the rest of the community to mete out punishment when rules are broken. Seasonal feast days establish the rhythms of the yearly calendar. Leviticus notes the commemoration of the first Passover, when God asks the Jewish people to mark their doorposts with blood so that they will remain unharmed, as well as the rules for celebrating with unleavened bread. The book also inaugurates Yom Kippur, or the Day of Atonement; the ritual fast practiced by the Jewish people thrives in modern times. The book also introduces the concept of paying for one's wrongdoings.

Leviticus, though technical in nature, stresses the importance of living a holy

thy neighbor as thyself." In order to remain worthy of the new land God has promised His people, they must live in piety and devotion, even in the most ordinary times.

Marking of the door with the letter Tau

THE BOOK OF
NUMBERS

THE BOOK OF NUMBERS DOCUMENTS TWO ATTEMPTS BY THE ISRAELITES
TO ENTER AND CLAIM CANAAN, THE PROMISED LAND. MOSES LEADS TWO
GROUPS, A GENERATION APART, BUT GOD BARS HIM FROM ENTERING HIMSELF.

The fourth book of the Bible takes its name from two censuses taken of the Israelites, one generation apart. God tells Moses and his brother, Aaron, to take a census of all men fit for military service. He specifies that they are to exempt the Levites from this

accounting, because they are required to help Aaron and his two remaining sons in their priestly duties.

Moses and Aaron receive two silver trumpets to lead them into battle after the celebration of the Second Passover. With the box that carries the Ten

*The census
at Bethlehem*

Commandments and the furnishings of the Sacred Tent at the head of their procession, the Israelites break camp, leaving the holy mountain of Sinai.

Numbers relates the frustrations, betrayals, complaints, and impatience God's people exhibit on their way to the Promised Land. It reinforces the rules of Leviticus and stresses the punishments and penalties for disobeying God. When, for example, the people complain bitterly about marching through the desert without enough meat, God sends them an abundance of quails, followed by an epidemic that kills everyone who voiced their dissatisfaction.

Reaching the border of Canaan, the Israelites send a cadre of spies into the land; most, hoping to prevent an invasion, come back with false reports. Only two tell the truth about the beautiful, fertile land to which God has lead His people, and when the majority of Israelites fearfully shirk their

God tells Moses to speak to a rock. Instead, Moses strikes it twice with his staff, producing water for the people. Yet, because he does not exactly follow

Moses striking the Rock

And Moses lifted up his hand, and with his rod he smote the rock twice: and the water came out abundantly, and the congregation drank, and their beasts also.

NUMBERS 20:11

orders to invade, God considers the entire generation lost. Declaring them unworthy of the land He is giving them, He orders his people to travel through the desert, living as shepherds until all who refused to fight die off. Even Moses and Aaron cannot escape God's wrath. In the desert, without water,

God's instructions and takes credit for this miracle, he learns that he will lead the people to Canaan, but never enter.

Numbers spans the length of forty years. At the end, Moses takes a new census of the next generation of Israelites, all willing to fight to enter Canaan and fulfill God's wishes.

NUMBERS IN THE BIBLE

Numerical patterns appear throughout the Bible,
lending structure and symbolism to some of the
text's most important themes.

NUMBERS DO NOT appear randomly in the Bible, but rather stand for a deeper spiritual meaning. Scholars continue to explore the hidden numerical messages in these sacred texts. Here, as an introduction, are some of the numbers that appear frequently, along with their biblical significance.

1 Absolute singleness, beginning, and unity.

2 Division, opposites/pairing: the Son has two natures, human and divine; two testaments; humankind is male and female.

3 Divine perfection, Godhead: the Father, Son, and Holy Spirit are also omniscient, omnipresent, omnipotent; three qualities of the universe, each of which are three in turn: time (past, present, future); space (height, width, depth); matter (solid, liquid, gas); thought, word, deed.

4 Creation of earth, cosmic order: Four directions (north, south, east, west); four phases of the moon.

5 Grace, redemption, teaching: five books of Moses; David picks up five smooth stones to fight Goliath; Jesus feeds five thousand with five barley loaves.

6 Man, God creates both man and snake on the sixth day, imperfection, disobedience.

The Dove sent forth from the Ark

Seven Saints: Francis, Lawrence, Cosmas, John the Baptist, Damian, Peter of Verona, John the Evangelist

7 Spiritual perfection; completeness as a sign of God; divine worship; obedience: used 562 times, including derivatives (seventh, sevens), most common in biblical prophecy.

8 New beginnings: eight humans allowed on Noah's ark, circumcision on the eighth day, God's eight covenants with Abraham.

10 Law, government, most common counting units (based on fingers and toes); restoration; the Ten Commandments.

11 Disorganization, disintegration: the 11 disciples of Jesus watch his betrayal by one; the eleventh hour; Genesis 11 (rebellion against God through the tower of Babel); John sees 11 things in connection with the Final Judgment.

12 Divine government, church, and God's authority: product of divine three and earthly four;

The Holy Trinity

12 Tribes of Israel; Jesus is 12 when he first appears in public and speaks at the Temple; 12 apostles; New Jerusalem measures 12,000 furlongs.

40 Testing, probation: forty days of rain during the flood; Moses and the Israelites wander forty years in the desert; Moses remains on Sinai forty days; Satan tempts Jesus for forty days and forty nights.

50 Celebration: the Jubilee follows year 49 (Leviticus 25:10); Pentecost occurs fifty days after Christ's resurrection, when the Holy Spirit first pours out upon the Church.

70 Human leadership and judgment: the product of two perfect numbers (seven and ten) represents divine perfect order.

The Wilderness

AFTER THE ISRAELITES REFUSE TO HONOR GOD'S DIRECTIVE THAT
THEY ENTER AND OVERTAKE THE PROMISED LAND, HE SUBJECTS
THEM TO A PERIOD OF FORTY YEARS IN A BARREN DESERT,
UNTIL A NEW GENERATION PROVES WILLING.

God leads the Israelites to the borders of Canaan—the land He has promised them since the time of Abraham—two years after their deliverance from Egypt. But when only two spies, Caleb and Joshua, return with truthful reports about fertile and beautiful Canaan, and the rest come back with lies meant to discourage the Israelites, they refuse to invade Canaan and do God's bidding, thereby incurring His wrath. As a result,

an outraged God decrees that, apart from Caleb and Joshua, those over the age of twenty will never enter the Promised Land; the tribe will wander in the desert until the reluctant die out—punishment for this cowardliness and faithlessness. The Israelites launch a futile invasion, attempting to appease God, but they suffer defeat without the Lord's support.

Moses bears the brunt of his people's complaints. Doomed to wander the desert for the next forty years, they blame him for leading them out of Egypt, a land with which they were familiar, to a life fraught with such perils and punishments as epidemics, fiery destruction, and the threat of being swallowed up by the earth.

Through these scenes the Bible covers the priestly duties of Aaron and the Levites,

The Jews in the Desert

including the Levites' directive to collect tithes from the community. As the people are dying of thirst, Moses performs a miracle to produce water but takes full credit for it. This display angers God, who tells Moses that although he will eventually be able to look on the Promised Land, he will never enter it. As they wander through the wilderness the Israelites fail to enter the Kingdom of Edom, though they eventually manage to conquer the Amorites, the residents of a neighboring, equally inhospitable kingdom.

Gaining confidence as they pass through these regions, they grow increasingly eager to enter the Promised Land. They next enter the Kingdom of Moab, where the king's seer predicts God will favor the Israelites. Beautiful women come forth to seduce the male Israelites, some of whom become pagans; many die in retribution. Moses oversees the second census, and after forty years of doubt, temptation, and hardship of every kind, God orders His chosen people to invade and take over Canaan.

The Israelites gathering Manna

OPPOSITE PAGE: *Moses and the messengers from Canaan*

MONEY AND MEASUREMENTS

The stories of the Bible span from the time when people first used coins as money to the development of more modern currencies, some of which are still in use today.

AS MONEY BECAME increasingly important, the Bible advised on its use and management. There are more than eight hundred scriptures dealing with money. The Bible lays out strict rules for lending, giving, tithing, paying fair wages, and investing, and it also inveighs against greed, price gouging, unjust business practices, and debt.

People did not use coins as money until about 500 BCE. Accordingly, in the Old Testament, a reference to the weight of silver (such as ten shekels of silver) is likely to refer to jewelry or ingots, not ten silver coins. The biblical units of weight include a talent, worth three thousand shekels, and the gerah, worth one twentieth

of a shekel. To establish trade between their nations, the Queen of Sheba gave King Solomon 120 talents of gold (360,000 shekels)—a fortune— in addition to a great quantity of spices and precious stones. Judah and his brothers sold Joseph into slavery for twenty shekels of silver ingots, which could buy ten rams.

Procession of the Queen of Sheba and meeting between the Queen of Sheba and King Solomon

> And he brought me thither, and, behold, *there was* a man,
> whose appearance *was* like the appearance of brass, with a line
> of flax in his hand, and a measuring reed; and he stood in the gate.
>
> EZEKIEL: 40:3

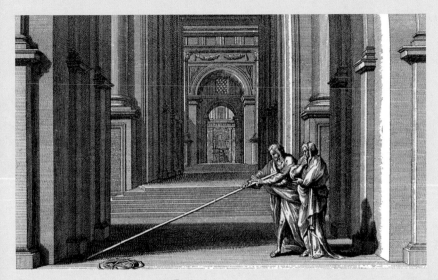
The measuring of a new temple in Ezekiel

In chapters 40–42 of Ezekiel, Ezekiel envisions a man with a measuring reed who gives exact instructions for building a new temple, including the length, in cubits, of every wall, gate, vestibule, priestly chamber, courtyard, and window. A cubit is between 18.9 and 22.7 inches in length; a measuring reed, taken from the calamus plant, is six cubits long. A handbreadth measures between 3.15 and 3.78 inches; a span was the equivalent of three handbreadths.

The New Testament names a variety of foreign coins that the Hebrews used, which had to be converted by money changers. One Greek drachma was the equivalent of a day laborer's wage. A Greek agurion equaled thirty Hebrew shekels, which was the official compensation for an accidentally slain servant, as well as the amount for which Judas betrayed Jesus. The smallest Jewish coin, a mite, equaled 1/128 of a drachma.

Approximating the load a donkey could carry determined dry measurements. The largest measurement, a homer (ten ephahs), equaled 220 liters, roughly eight bushels; the smallest, a cab, equaled roughly 1/18 of an ephah.

Measurements for length and distance tended to center on aspects of the human body. A mile was the distance one could walk in 18 minutes; a parsang was the distance one could walk in 72 minutes.

Silver tridrachm from Corinth

THE BOOK OF
DEUTERONOMY

DEUTERONOMY IS ONE OF SEVERAL BOOKS IN THE BIBLE THAT LARGELY
SERVES TO EMPHASIZE THEMES, LAWS, AND HISTORY ALREADY COVERED
ELSEWHERE. IT CONTAINS THE SHEMA, A CENTRAL PRAYER IN JUDAISM.

Moses considered the first commandment—that there is only one God and He, alone, must be obeyed—the greatest. In the fifth and final book of the Torah, Moses recounts his past forty years leading the Israelites. On the brink of invading Canaan, about to realize the promise God made to Abraham, the Israelites recall the covenant they have with God—how He has rescued, loved, and blessed them—and the importance of keeping their end of the bargain by obeying His laws.

Based on the Greek word *deuteronomion*, which translates as "second law," Deuteronomy essentially repeats the laws, rules, history, and rituals contained in Exodus, Leviticus, and Numbers. Moses reminds the

Moses on Mount Sinai

Israelites, in three separate addresses, of their freedom from slavery, their wanderings in the desert, and their recent military victories near the border of Canaan. He also reminds them that their past complaints and lack of faith angers God and that they are taking over Canaan not because they are good, but because the people in Canaan are evil and have displeased God. Moses stresses, again, that as long as they obey God's rules they will be allowed to remain in the Promised Land. If they do not, they run the risk of being scattered across many nations.

Moses devotes his second discourse to the importance of the Ten Commandments, which he reiterates and explains at length. He stresses the significance of setting up a house of

Moses's final words before pronouncing a blessing on the Twelve Tribes of Israel are about the importance of obeying

Gleaning a wheat field after harvest

When thou cuttest down thine harvest in thy field, and hast forgot a sheaf in the field, thou shalt not go again to fetch it: it shall be for the stranger, for the fatherless, and for the widow: that the Lord thy God may bless thee in all the work of thine hands.

DEUTERONOMY 24:19

worship, as well as the consequences of not keeping God's laws. Religious festivals and legal principles define both Jewish religion and culture. Moses reminds the people, again, of God's covenant with Israel.

In Deuteronomy, as in Numbers, God declares Joshua to be Moses's successor.

God. The Lord takes Moses to the top of a mountain, where he is able to see the future home of the nation of Israel before dying in the Land of Moab. The people mourn Moses, praising him as a great prophet: "And there arose not a prophet since in Israel like unto Moses, whom the Lord knew face to face."

BIBLICAL LAW

God handed Moses the Ten Commandments. Displayed publicly, these laws form the foundation of God's expectations for His people and continue to influence culture and the law in modern Western society.

THE TEN COMMANDMENTS, carved in stone and brought down from Mount Sinai by Moses, are still considered an essential underpinning of Western social, moral, and economic order. They summarize the plethora of scriptural law governing virtually every aspect of life and are the bedrock on which contemporary codes of jurisprudence rest. Biblical justice, as opposed to its secular antecedents, prescribes exact rules for preserving the

Descent From Mount Sinai

sacred and secular rights of others so that everyone is treated fairly. God's moral code makes each individual personally responsible for upholding the expectations of civil society. No

laws (borrowing, buying and selling, taxes, just weights and measures); labor (work ethic, God's work); servants and employees (duties of masters and workers); the keeping of

> And he wrote on the tables, according to the first writing, the ten commandments, which the Lord spake unto you in the mount out of the midst of the fire in the day of the assembly: and the Lord gave them unto me.
>
> DEUTERONOMY 10:4

Moses holds the Ten Commandments

longer do we live according to the whims of a human ruler—we each have our own personal relationship with God and must answer to Him above all.

The Bible provides guidance through parable and direct command on these aspects of life: one's relationship to God (faith, fear, love, worship, obedience) and proper methods of religious observance; the duties and qualifications of priests; dietary laws (forbidden foods, fasting); marriage and divorce (spousal duties, prohibited acts); family (inheritance and birthright, parental responsibility, child behavior); property rights; monetary

slaves; animal regulations (care of, use for labor, compensation for damage); government (leadership, judges, obligations); capital crimes (murder, sorcery, offenses against God, treason, sexual immorality); and warfare (rules of conduct toward enemies, permissible reasons for war, peace, and victory).

People consider physical display of the laws crucial to their observance. When God gives Moses the Ten Commandments in Exodus, He orders them to be displayed. Deuteronomy clearly states that the law must be publicly written, displayed, and recorded; every seven years the law is to be read aloud in public.

In the Bible, judges are a unique and important part of government. The surrounding nations are ruled by kings, but the Israelites alone, in addition to venerating their rulers, believe their judges are divinely inspired. Their ability to interpret God's law earns them much respect— for although it is possible to have a stable nation with corrupt leaders and citizens, as long as the judiciary remains pure, it will uphold the law.

The Shema

THE SHEMA IS A COLLECTION OF PASSAGES FROM THE OLD TESTAMENT THAT HOLDS A SPECIAL PLACE FOR JEWS. THE ULTIMATE EXPRESSION OF GOD'S LINK TO THE JEWISH PEOPLE, THE SHEMA IS ESPECIALLY IMPORTANT DURING YOM KIPPUR AND TO THE DYING.

Hear, O Israel, the Lord our God *is* one Lord:
And thou shalt love the Lord thy God with all thine heart,
and with all thy soul and with all thy might.
And these words, which I command thee this day, shall be in thine heart:
And thou shall teach them diligently unto thy children, and thou shalt
talk of them when thou sittest in thine house, and when thou walkest
by the way, and when thou liest down, and when thou risest up.
And thou shall bind them for a sign upon thine hand,
and they shall be as frontlets between thine eyes.
And thou shall write them upon the posts of thy house, and on thy gates.

DEUTERONOMY 6:4–9

These lines from Deuteronomy, the first words Moses recites to his people, contain the essence of the Jewish faith. Recited as a prayer twice a day, in the morning and again at night, they are the first words a child learns to read and write in Hebrew.

Addressed to the individual, Jews traditionally recite this first portion of the Shema near the end of Yom Kippur services. The dying invoke the Shema as a final declaration of faith. The second part of the Shema, found in Deuteronomy 11:13–21, addresses the Hebrew nation as a whole, outlining the rewards the faithful will earn by following God's commandments and warning of the severe retribution that God metes out to those who abandon Him. This section ends with a renewed command to recite daily the prayer, "Hear, O Israel," and to make sure that future generations respect its eternal importance.

Appearing in Numbers 15:37–41, the third part of the Shema is practical in nature, quoting God's command to His people to wear fringes on their garments. These fringes, the Bible says, will serve to remind all who see them to follow God's commandments. This section ends with the words, "I *am* the Lord your God, which brought you out of the land of Egypt, to be your God: I *am* the Lord your God." God thus tells His people that he will always bring them together, across the earth, wherever they happen to reside.

Jews praying in the Synagogue on Yom Kippur

CRIME AND PUNISHMENT

Along with God's promise through Moses to protect His people, He demands specific and sometimes harsh justice in response to the most serious crimes. In the New Testament, Jesus passes more lenient judgment but still promotes God's laws.

IN GENESIS 6, GOD HIMSELF extinguishes all humanity for their wickedness: "I will destroy man whom I have created from the face of the earth; both man, and beast, and the creeping thing, and the fowls of the air; for it repenteth me that I have made them." He spares Noah and his family, but after the flood, God states His principle regarding capital punishment: "Whoso sheddeth man's blood, by man shall his blood be shed" (Genesis 9:6). The death sentence also applies to those who hire another person to kill for them. If one commits manslaughter, however, or accidentally kills another, the appropriate punishment is banishment to a biblical City of Refuge.

Through Moses, God declares additional crimes punishable by death, including striking one's mother or father, kidnapping, witchcraft, Sabbath-breaking, idolatry, adultery, rape, incest, blasphemy, and false prophecy.

Biblical law demands that no one be condemned without the testimony under oath of at least two witnesses in front of the accused. The sentence must follow strict guidelines according to God's word, not the judge's discretion.

The First Mourning

The stoning of Achan

I also will do this unto you; I will even appoint over you terror, consumption, and the burning ague, that shall consume the eyes, and cause sorrow of heart: and ye shall sow your seed in vain, for your enemies shall eat it."

In the New Testament, Jesus practices flexibility with Old Testament law, as in the story of the condemned adulteress in John 8. The scribes and Pharisees bring her before Jesus to receive the Old Testament punishment that fits her crime—death by stoning. Jesus remarks, "He that is without sin among you, let him first cast a stone at her." After the men have all crept away He asks the woman, "Where are those thine accusers? Hath no man condemned thee? . . . Neither do I condemn thee: go, and sin no more."

Christ and the Adulteress

Various punishments may be inflicted: stoning, whipping, hanging, burning, beheading, dismemberment, or banishment. For crimes of property, such as stealing livestock, the judge may demand confiscation of goods, compensation, and restitution for lost time, property damage, or injury.

In Leviticus 26, God warns His people: "If ye shall despise my statutes, or if your soul abhor my judgments, so that ye will not do all my commandments, but that ye break my covenant:

The
Historical Books

The second section of the Old Testament covers eight hundred years of the history of the Israelites and consists of 12 books: Joshua, Judges, Ruth, 1 Samuel, 2 Samuel, 1 Kings, 2 Kings, 1 Chronicles, 2 Chronicles, Ezra, Nehemiah, and Esther. Written out of sequence at different times and later chronologically combined, they relate the cycles of success, failure, apostasy, deportation, ruination, and rebuilding of Jerusalem by God's people. Beginning with Joshua and his successful invasion and division of the Holy Land, the Historical Books detail the dark ages of the Israelites, their descent into anarchy, and their need for strong leadership. God's rejection of Saul, the first king of the Israelites, demonstrates the Lord's expectation of obedience and marks an important milestone in the rise of the Israelites' monarchy. David expands the kingdom, and his son Solomon creates the great temple that raises Jerusalem to the peak of her glory. Yet, a cycle of division, decline, and collapse follows—the consequences of sin and faithlessness. Ignoring the prophets, the people suffer banishment and domination. As the Historical Books end, the Israelites repent and, free from exile, return to the land God gave them.

The victory of Joshua over the Amalekites

THE BOOK OF
JOSHUA

THE BOOK OF JOSHUA IS THE STORY OF GOD'S PEOPLE CONQUERING THE PROMISED LAND. THEY FOLLOW JOSHUA INTO CANAAN AND DIVIDE THE LAND AMONG THE TWELVE TRIBES NAMED FOR THE SONS OF ISRAEL.

Named for Moses's successor, Joshua, the first of the Historical Books, serves as a bridge from the laws and promises detailed in Deuteronomy. Joshua tells of the successful conquering of the land of Canaan and its division among the Twelve Tribes. It also demonstrates how God honors his agreement, spanning back to the days of Abraham, to give this Promised Land to his people.

As the book opens, God commands Joshua to conquer Canaan. Resolute

> And they answered Joshua, saying, All that thou commandest us we will do, and whithersoever thou sendest us, we will go.
>
> JOSHUA 1:16

An ivory plaque depicting scenes from the Story of Joshua

and confident, Joshua knows that his power comes from God; as long as he and his people have faith, they will succeed. After miraculously crossing the Jordan River, Joshua oversees the circumcision of all the desert-born men. They celebrate Passover, and, for the first time, the Israelites eat food produced on their new land. Joshua meets an angel of the Lord and God instructs him to bring down the walls of Jericho. The successful destruction of this great city inspires fear of Joshua and his people in all the kingdoms of Canaan. After overrunning the city of Ai and killing its thousands of inhabitants, Joshua sets up an altar on Mount Ebal. Here, he places the Ark of the Covenant, which holds the Ten

Commandments. After administering a blessing to his people, he reads aloud the whole Law of Moses and announces the consequences and punishments for straying from these commandments.

Throughout his life, Joshua periodically expands the conquered territory for the Israelites. Always successful, he moves only at the behest of God. When Joshua conquers all the land that God promised the Israelites, the people break up the territories into twelve sections, one for each of the Twelve Tribes. Happily settled in their new land, God's people enjoy a rare time of peace.

Before he dies, Joshua gathers all his people together to remind them of God's covenant with Abraham, whose own father was an idol merchant. Joshua reminds them that, in return for honoring the one God, they are now the beneficiaries of His faith as descendants of Abraham. The people promise never to worship other gods,

and Joshua implores them never to forget their pledge. After Joshua's death, the Israelites retrieve the remains of Joseph from Egypt and bury them in the land they have reclaimed.

Joshua commanding the sun to stand still upon Gibeon

ARK OF THE COVENANT

Moses and Joshua in the Tabernacle

THE BOOK OF EXODUS first describes the Ark of the Covenant as a chest containing the stone tablets on which the Ten Commandments are inscribed. Later books also list Aaron's rod, a jar of manna, and the first Torah scroll as contents of this golden vessel.

The chest, also known as the Ark of the Testimony and the Ark of God, was said to have accompanied the Israelites during much of their wanderings, until they either hid it or it was seized by the Babylonians during the destruction of Jerusalem and the Temple of Solomon.

Entry into the Promised Land

GOD VISITS JOSHUA AND COMMANDS HIM TO LEAD HIS PEOPLE INTO THE PROMISED LAND. AFTER A MIRACULOUS JOURNEY ACROSS THE JORDAN RIVER, JOSHUA'S PEOPLE FIGHT THE CANAANITES FOR THE LAND.

After the death of Moses, God speaks to Joshua and tells him that the time has come for him to lead his people into Canaan, the Promised Land. God assures Joshua of His full support, and Joshua relays this determination and strength to all of his people.

Before invading Canaan, Joshua sends two spies into the land. A prostitute named Rahab, who lives in a house set in the city wall of Jericho, assists in their hiding. She promises her full cooperation in exchange for the protection of her family in the coming battle.

The people of Canaan, familiar with tales of the power of the God of the Israelites, begin to fear the invasion. Once Joshua receives a positive report from his spies, he mobilizes his people to cross the Jordan River. Promising them many miracles to come, he asks the priests carrying the Ark of the Covenant containing the Ten Commandments to step into the river. The waters immediately stop flowing, allowing the priests and the Twelve Tribes of Israel to cross over to Canaan on the other side. When everyone has made safe passage, the Jordan begins flowing again. When the Canaanite kings learn of this miracle, it further dilutes their courage and instills in them even greater fear.

To revitalize the Covenant of Abraham, the Lord orders Joshua to circumcise the youngest generation of men born during the Israelites' exile in the desert. Later, the manna from Heaven that sustained the pilgrims throughout their wanderings disappears. The Twelve Tribes

Moses shown the Promised Land

of Israel celebrate their first Passover in the Promised Land, eating food grown in the soil of their new country.

With God's help, Joshua and his soldiers destroy entire cities, realizing amazing military victories throughout Canaan. His people wipe out whole kingdoms, leaving no one alive, assuring that they will never mix with the Canaanites in any way or be tempted to worship other gods. Unlike Moses, God spares Joshua the burden of an insubordinate or faithless people. By the time the Twelve Tribes finally arrive in Canaan, they are eager to accept the land that has long been promised to them and are determined to fight for it.

Episode in the Life of Joshua

The Angel of Death and the First Passover

Jericho

GOD SPEAKS TO JOSHUA AND PLACES THE LEGENDARY CITY OF JERICHO INTO HIS HANDS. JOSHUA ORDERS THE ISRAELITE PRIESTS TO CIRCLE THE CITY. IN THE SPAN OF SEVEN DAYS THEY PENETRATE ITS WALLS AND DESTROY THE CITY.

With its high walls and strong fortifications, the city of Jericho was legendary for its power, wealth, and invulnerability. Along with its formidable king and brave army, Jericho seemed to be impervious to any assault, be it physical or spiritual.

After their first Passover in Canaan, Joshua meets a man with a sword near the city. When Joshua asks if he is an enemy or one of his soldiers, the man replies that he is neither. Instead he says he is the commander of the Lord's army and orders Joshua to take off his sandals, as he stands on holy ground.

Shortly after this curious incident, God informs Joshua

The Fall of Jericho

that he is about to put the city of Jericho under his control. He orders Joshua's army of Israelites to march around the walls of Jericho once a day for six days, and seven times on the seventh day. God instructs seven priests to lead them, each blowing a ram's-horn trumpet; with them they carry the Ark of the Covenant. On the seventh day, the group again proceeds to march around Jericho six times in this same way; before the seventh pass, Joshua tells his people that God has granted them Jericho.

Once inside its walls they destroy every resident—except for the prostitute Rahab and her family, who aided Joshua's spies.

The Seven Trumpets of Jericho

According to God's instructions, when the army hears the trumpeters play a single long note, they are to shout as they witness the walls of Jericho collapse. The victorious Israelites install Rahab and her family as members of their people while sparing no other living thing, neither livestock nor children. God tells the Israelites to take nothing from the city except for objects made of gold, silver, bronze, and iron, which are marked for placement in the Lord's Treasury. The soldiers then burn conquered Jericho to the ground, and Joshua warns that the Lord will curse anyone who tries to rebuild the city.

Joshua realizes the full cooperation and faith of his people is crucial to his success at Jericho. Though he is the designated military leader of the Israelites, he credits the power of God for his exceptional victories, never wavering in his faith or questioning God's wish that the Chosen People go to battle and receive this land on which to settle.

The Walls of Jericho fall down

The Twelve Tribes of Israel

EACH OF THE TWELVE TRIBES WERE NAMED FOR A DESCENDANT
OF JACOB. THESE DESCENDANTS FOLLOWED JOSHUA
INTO CANAAN AND FOUGHT BESIDE HIM TO CLAIM THE LAND.

After Jacob—son of Isaac and grandson of Abraham—wrestles with the angel, God renames him Israel, which means "to struggle with the divine." He has 12 sons, who will become known as the ancestors of the Twelve Tribes of Israel: Asher, Benjamin, Dan, Gad, Issachar, Joseph, Judah, Levi, Naphtali, Reuben, Simeon, and Zebulun.

When Joseph's eleven brothers and their families first came to live with him in Egypt, they numbered seventy. By the time of the Exodus, hundreds of years later, the Twelve Tribes are said to number 600,000. These are the people who follow Moses out of Egypt—and it is their immediate descendants who follow Joshua into Canaan.

When all of Canaan has been conquered, God orders Joshua to divide up the land, giving a portion to each of the Twelve Tribes. The Levites, now the priestly class, will, instead of land, receive a portion of the offerings given to the Lord. The descendants of the sons of Joseph, Ephraim and Manasseh, each receive portions of land in their father's honor.

This united Kingdom of Israel remains intact for approximately three hundred years, until Solomon's son, Rehoboam, loses the allegiance of the northern part of the kingdom, after which

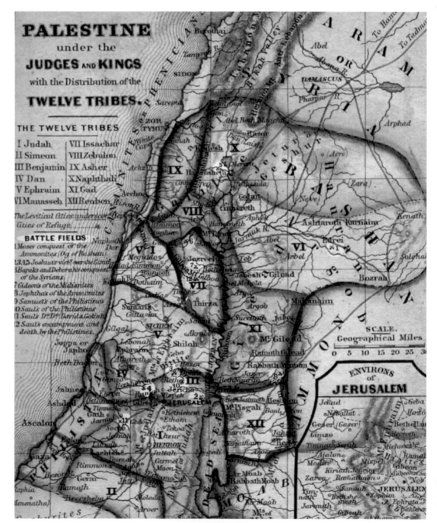

A nineteenth-century map showing the land granted to each of the Twelves Tribes

Benjamites take women of Shiloh as wives

only the tribes of Judah and Benjamin remain loyal to him.

The other ten tribes form a new country, the Northern Kingdom of Israel. Judah and Benjamin call their country Judah, and they regard it as superior, because it contains Jerusalem and the Temple of Solomon. The northern tribes have no access to the temple, so many Levite priests also move to Judah. When Assyria overruns Israel in 722 BCE, the inhabitants disperse or experience deportation at the hands of the Assyrians. In 586 BCE, Babylon takes Judah captive and exiles its most important citizens.

In 537 BCE, the exiles in Babylon begin slowly returning to a much smaller Judah. Having preserved the purity of their religious practices during captivity, they do not mix with the natives who call themselves "Hebrews," for they had married into foreign tribes and incorporated neighboring religious practices into their worship. The returnees refer to these people as "Samaritans," while "Jew"

The Twelve Tribes of Israel

specifically connotes a returnee from Judah. No longer organized by tribes, the biblical peoples delineate family background along the lines of clans.

THE BOOK OF
JUDGES

IN THE BOOK OF JUDGES, GOD'S PEOPLE MIX WITH THE NATIVE
TRIBES OF CANAAN. CONSEQUENTLY, THEY ABANDON THEIR FAITH
AND DRIVE THE PROMISED LAND INTO CHAOS.

T he seventh book of the Bible is called Judges, in reference to several heroic figures who assume responsibility for leadership of the Israelite nation during its darkest hour. God, repeatedly insulted and forsaken, looms large throughout this cyclical saga of disobedience and repentance, which spans generations.

The book opens with the death of Joshua, the great leader who leaves behind the people he so triumphantly

The triumphant commander Jephthah sees his daughter

unified. Just one generation later, the Tribes of Israel have started to fragment. Against God's wishes, they assimilate into the numerous native tribes of Canaan—peoples the Lord ordered them to drive out and destroy—gradually adapting native religious practices. When they stop serving God altogether, He vows that He will no longer aid His ungrateful people in battle. Cycles of domination and oppression follow—various foreign kings besiege the Israelites, and they beseech their God for forgiveness and help.

Though His people consistently betray Him, God continues to reward them when they renew their covenant. Over many years, in different parts of the nation, He inspires wise leaders from various walks of life ("judges"), who help His people rediscover their true identity. We meet successful military commanders, such as Othniel and Ehud,

Gideon's Army

throughout the land; the Israelites forget the many previous injunctions of Moses. The brutal rape of a Levite priest's concubine ignites a war

And the Lord said unto him, Surely I will be with thee, and thou shalt smite the Midianites as one man.

JUDGES 6:16

as well as the prophetess Deborah, who serves as a counselor and mediator for her people. The hero Gideon defeats the Midianites, bringing forty years of peace to the land—only to see his evil son, Abimelech, destroy the harmony. Samson, too, takes an unexpected route to victory over the Philistines.

By the end of Judges, chaos reigns. Corrupt religious practices take root

between the people of Benjamin and the other Tribes of Israel. All sides lament the rift and experience anguish as they fracture the unity of their own people, nearly destroying the nation. The last lines of Judges express the need for strong leadership: "In those days *there was* no king in Israel: every man did *that which was* right in his own eyes."

Deborah and Gideon

DEBORAH AND GIDEON, THOUGH OF DIFFERENT GENERATIONS, BOTH PROPHESIED AND FOUGHT TO BRING PEACE TO ISRAEL.

One of the most powerful women in the Bible, Deborah was known as a great prophet and judge. She would sit under a palm tree, and her people came to seek her counsel in all things. After she prophesies that the military leader Barak will defeat the Canaanite king in battle, she sings a poetic song about the Israelites' subsequent victory.

Battle of Gideon against the Midianites

Deborah the Prophetess

In it she describes the dire living conditions that result from oppression and tells how God inspired her to encourage the revolt. She praises those who fought, but most of all she thanks God for this victory, which marks the start of another forty years of peace.

The next generation, again, falls into sin and oppression. The Midianites have conquered the Israelites. Gideon, a young man from the Manasseh tribe, after crying out to God, comes to their rescue, first destroying the altar to foreign gods set up by his own father and subsequently enlisting neighboring Israelite tribes to aid him in battle. Taking his war plan directly from God—who creates such confusion on the battlefield that the enemy soldiers accidentally kill one another—Gideon declares God the ruler of Israel. Again, there are forty years of peace.

Jephthah and Samson

JEPHTHAH AND SAMSON WERE JUDGES, BOTH KNOWN
FOR THEIR PROWESS AND STRENGTH, WHO WOULD
EACH ENCOUNTER TRAGEDY.

The Ammonites overran the territories of the Tribes of Israel during another period in which they ignored the laws of Moses. They beseech God for help and He sends them Jephthah, a great soldier from Gilead; they agree to make him their leader. In exchange for a victory, Jephthah vows to the Lord to make a burnt offering of the first person he sees after returning from battle. Successful, Jephthah goes home, where he encounters his only daughter. Despondent and aggrieved, he keeps his vow and slays her.

By the time Samson is born, the Israelites had been under the rule of the Philistines for forty years. Prophesied to be the deliverer of his people, Samson is a Nazirite, a religious person who neither drinks alcohol nor shaves his hair.

The strongest person anyone has ever seen, Samson wipes out thousands of Philistines single-handedly. He falls in love with Delilah, who discovers the source of his strength—his hair—and cuts it off, betraying Samson.

The Philistines blind him and make him a slave. Yet when his captors parade him in front of a massive crowd, he brings down the temple walls, killing the Philistines and himself.

The death of Samson

THE BOOK OF
RUTH

RUTH'S GOODNESS AND UNERRING DESIRE TO EMBRACE
THE CULTURE AND ALMIGHTY GOD OF THE ISRAELITES GRANTS
HER A SPECIAL PLACE IN THE OLD TESTAMENT.

Though it takes place in the lawless and godless time of Judges, the eighth book of the Bible offers a peaceful respite from the punishment, betrayal, and violence endemic to that period. Named for its main character, the Book of Ruth espouses the virtues of loyalty and devotion and the willingness of a woman of non-Israelite heritage to follow God. Indeed, even as those born under God's protection seem to constantly take it for granted, Ruth, a Moabite woman, yearns to live within God's laws.

As the book opens, a family from the clan of Ephrath moves out of

Naomi entreating Ruth and Orpah to return to the Land of Moab

Bethlehem at a rare time of peace between the Tribes of Israel and Moab. When the patriarch Elimelech dies, his wife, Naomi, and their two sons remain in the foreign land of Moab. Both sons marry Moabite women, Orpah and Ruth. When her two sons die, leaving their widows childless, Naomi decides to return to Bethlehem. She encourages her daughters-in-law to go back to their families and cultures and resume their lives. Orpah reluctantly follows this advice; Ruth refuses, insisting it is her duty to accompany her mother-in-law back to her country and care for her.

Though she receives a warm welcome from her family, Naomi is bitter about returning without anything to show for her life in Moab. In order to care for Naomi, Ruth works in a field, harvesting grain. Boaz, the owner of the field, is one of Naomi's relatives. Praising Ruth for her loyalty, he makes sure the other

Ruth in Boaz's field

son, Obed, her first grandchild. The book ends with a description of the future generations to come after Obed; the son of Jesse and Obed's grandson, will become David, Israel's great leader and king.

As a humble foreigner, Ruth offers a perfect example of the redemption awaiting those who accept God's protection. Acting out of her innate

---

And Ruth said, Intreat me not to leave thee, *or* to return from following after thee: for whither thou goest, I will go; and where thou lodgest, I will lodge: thy people *shall be* my people, and thy God my God.

RUTH 1:16

---

workers treat her well. Eventually, Naomi arranges for Ruth to marry Boaz, a relationship he welcomes, owing to Ruth's many wonderful qualities. Much to Naomi's joy, Ruth and Boaz have a

goodness, Ruth not only improves the life of her mother-in-law, she also enriches the entire nation of Israel as the great-grandmother of one of its greatest leaders.

THE FIRST AND SECOND BOOKS OF

SAMUEL

THE PROPHET SAMUEL HELPS TO GUIDE THE WAR-PLAGUED PEOPLE OF ISRAEL TO A TIME OF PEACE. CONCERNED FOR THEIR FUTURE AFTER SAMUEL, THE PEOPLE ASK GOD FOR A MONARCH TO LEAD THEM.

Originally one volume, the ninth and tenth books of the Bible detail the transition from the days of the judges, who carefully guide Israel with their wisdom, to the eventual installation of a monarchy. The book, named for the last great judge, begins with the birth of the prophet Samuel. His mother, Hannah, has trouble conceiving, and, once pregnant, she joyfully promises her son to the Lord. In Shiloh, Samuel is raised by Eli, a high priest. Samuel becomes a revered prophet who speaks directly to God, and, by the time he reaches adulthood, people across Israel seek his advice. It is Samuel who is directly responsible for establishing the monarchy of Israel's first king, Saul, and his successor, David.

First Samuel depicts a country frequently at war with its neighbors. When the Philistines capture the Israelites' sacred Ark of the Covenant during battle, God unleashes a horrible plague upon the Philistines to force its return. Under Samuel's leadership, and thanks to his ability to communicate directly with God, the people enjoy a time of peace. As Samuel ages, they worry about their future; eventually, they decide to forfeit God's direct rule and appoint an earthly king. Though Samuel warns of the pitfalls that come along with a human monarch, the people pressure him to ask God for assistance in finding a ruler. God chooses Saul to be the first king of Israel, imbuing him with divine energy. Following a major success in battle, the entire country unites around him.

Saul ignores Samuel's warnings that a king must always follow God, and God exhibits His displeasure, challenging his occupation of the throne. David, a young shepherd, succeeds Saul. Though anointed by Samuel, a jealous Saul proceeds to attack David for years before he fully accepts God's mandate.

Second Samuel is devoted to the reign of King David. After Saul's death in battle, David defeats Saul's supporters to become king. He extends the borders of Israel, and though he is a God-loving man, he is not immune to grave errors and sin. After an adulterous affair with Bathsheba, his reign experiences scores of problems.

OPPOSITE PAGE:
Death of King Saul

Life of Samuel

SAMUEL IS RAISED BY A PRIEST AFTER HIS MOTHER DEDICATES
HIM TO GOD. HE RELAYS GOD'S MESSAGES DIRECTLY TO THE PEOPLE,
TRAVELING THE LAND AND SETTLING VARIOUS DISPUTES.

The first great prophet born in the nation of Israel, Samuel communicates directly with God, spreading His dedicate her firstborn to God's service. The high priest Eli raises Samuel at Shiloh, and Samuel grows famous all over Israel

The infant Samuel

> That the Lord called Samuel:
> and he answered, Here *am* I.
>
> 1 SAMUEL 3:4

word to the people. Universally respected as a leader, like Moses before him, he anoints the first kings of Israel but voices grave misgivings about instituting a monarchic system.

His mother, Hannah, implores God for a child, promising to for his wisdom and prophetic skill. Aside from being an astute judge, Samuel leads his people, with God's guidance, to a great military victory over the Philistines. He becomes a ruler of Israel in a time of peace, known for visiting far-flung

territories and settling disputes. Though the people love Samuel, they know his sons are corrupt judges; accordingly, they beg God to install a king so that, like the people of the nations surrounding them, they could enjoy truly strong leadership.

When God orders Samuel to anoint Saul as the Israelites' first king, he obeys—but only after stressing how important it is for the king to follow God's orders.

Saul reproved by Samuel
for not obeying the
Commandments of the Lord

Life of Saul

SAUL IS ANOINTED THE FIRST MONARCH OF ISRAEL.
SAUL FALLS ON HIS SWORD IN BATTLE AFTER FAILING TO HEED
ALL OF GOD'S RULES, FULFILLING THE PROPHECY OF SAMUEL.

Saul—tall and handsome, the son of a wealthy man named Kish—seems an ideal choice for Israel's first king. Saul and his servant, searching the land for Kish's donkeys, decide to ask the prophet Samuel for help in locating them. When Saul comes into view, Samuel hears the Lord's voice say, "It is he who shall be king." After Samuel anoints Saul with oil, Saul's bearing and attitude change, as he is filled with God.

The people unite behind Saul after he defeats the Ammonites, proving himself in warfare.

Yet God rebukes Saul when he neglects to follow all of God's instructions in battle. Saul clings to his status as monarch, despite the warnings of Samuel. God plagues Saul with agitation and mental fits; he goes on to summon David, who plays his harp to soothe him. Eventually, realizing David is a formidable rival, Saul makes several unsuccessful attempts to kill him.

Contravening his own rules prohibiting sorcery, Saul asks a witch to summon the ghost of Samuel, who predicts his demise in battle the next day. Saul dies along with his three sons, falling on his own sword.

The suicide of Saul

Life of David

SECRETLY NAMED SECOND KING OF ISRAEL, DAVID INTEGRATES HIMSELF INTO THE ROYAL FAMILY. HE FLEES IN THE FACE OF SAUL'S JEALOUSY, RETURNING UPON SAUL'S SON'S DEATH TO UNIFY JUDAH AND ISRAEL AS ONE KINGDOM.

God chose David—shepherd, musician, poet, and warrior—to rule over Israel because he was a better representative of its people than the deeply flawed King Saul.

A great-grandson of Ruth the Moabite, we first encounter David tending his sheep in Bethlehem. The prophet Samuel searches him out, secretly anointing him to be the second King of Israel.

King Saul refuses to give up his throne, later experiencing mental fits, courtesy of an evil spirit. As a result, he summons David to his palace to play the harp, which soothes him. David further ingratiates himself with the royal family when he defeats the giant Goliath in a one-on-one battle to determine the victor in a war with the Philistines. Saul rewards him with an appointment as commander of his troops.

David enjoys a close friendship with Saul's son Jonathan and marries Saul's daughter, Michal. David is successful in whatever he does because he has God's favor. Saul grows jealous, and he attempts to murder David several times. With the help of Michal and Jonathan, David avoids death, eventually fleeing the land while seeking support in every town he travels through. Saul intensifies his persecution of David, forcing Michal to take

David with the head of Goliath

another husband. Because he respects Saul's place as the first appointed king of Israel, David, them all. Upon David's return, the people declare him the king of Judah. Ish-bosheth, one of

---

And he said to David, Thou *art* more righteous than I: for thou hast rewarded me good, whereas I have rewarded thee evil.

1 SAMUEL 24:17

---

on two separate occasions, refuses the opportunity to kill him.

When Saul and three of his sons die in a battle on Mount Gilboa, David sincerely mourns

Saul's surviving sons, inherits the Kingdom of Israel.

After Ish-bosheth's demise, the people of Israel elevate David to the throne and he combines the two kingdoms.

David and Jonathan

After driving the Philistines out of Jerusalem, David establishes a central system of governance and builds a large palace there. The prophet Nathan promises him that his dynasty will never end. Nonetheless, David brings strife to his own house by falling in love with Bathsheba and arranging for the killing of her husband in battle so that he can take her as his wife. The country revolts, and David runs from the city he made great. Upon his eventual return, his son, Solomon, becomes king.

King David in prayer

JERUSALEM

Jerusalem existed for two thousand years before King David conquered it for the Kingdom of Israel. At the time of the kingdom's fall, Jerusalem stood as Judah's capital city, remaining strong until the Romans leveled it in 70 CE.

FIRST MENTIONED BY NAME in Joshua 10:1, the Bible references Jerusalem more than six hundred times thereafter (it also appears as "Yerushalayim").

Archeologists estimate that the city existed for two thousand years before it became the capital of the Jewish nation, as well as a political and religious center, after King David conquered it in 1000 BCE.

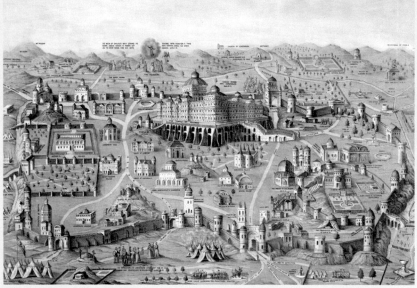

The ancient city of Jerusalem with Solomon's Temple

Abraham and Melchizedek

Genesis 14:18, in which it is called "Salem," contains the first biblical reference to this city. Abraham travels there to pay tithes to Melchizadek, who is called the high priest and king of Salem. Later, in Genesis 22:2, Abraham nearly sacrifices his son at Mount Moriah, subsequently the Temple Mount in the time of Solomon. King Solomon's great temple, as well as his palace, made Jerusalem a respected city throughout the ancient world.

When the Kingdom of Israel broke with the south, Jerusalem remained the capital of Judah, its temple considered the house of God. The Babylonians destroyed much of the city in 586 BCE, razing the temple and the city

> If I forget thee, O Jerusalem, let my right hand forget her cunning.
> If I do not remember thee, let my tongue cleave to the roof
> of my mouth; if I prefer not Jerusalem above my chief joy.
>
> PSALMS 137:5–6

walls; when the exiles returned in 516 BCE, they constructed a new temple and rebuilt the city. In 37 BCE, King Herod famously expanded the ancient structure to great international acclaim. Yet, after the Romans leveled it while putting down a rebellion in 70 CE, Jerusalem degenerated into a minor Roman outpost. Today, all that remains of the great temple is the Western Wall, one of Judaism's holiest sites.

In the New Testament, Christ, as a child, visits Jerusalem for religious festivals. He is lost for three days until His parents find Him in the temple, arguing with the elders. It is here, too, that He is crucified, dies, and is buried. He ascends into heaven from the Mount of Olives, a few miles outside the city center.

The Pentecost—the descent of the Holy Spirit to the apostles—also occurs in Jerusalem. The Book of Revelations predicts that the New Jerusalem will be the center of the world again, a city free from sin, where God dwells.

Biblical Jerusalem and the great temple

The siege and destruction of Jerusalem by the Romans under the command of Titus, 70 CE

THE FIRST AND SECOND BOOKS OF
KINGS

COMPILED AS ONE BOOK AND LATER SPLIT INTO TWO—POSSIBLY DUE TO ITS SHEER SIZE—KINGS INTENDS TO CATALOG THE COMPLETE HISTORY OF EVERY RULER OF ISRAEL AND JUDAH.

The eleventh and twelfth books of the Bible, which tell of the greatness of King David and the glory of his son, Solomon, portray God's people as a strong and unified nation, blessed with prosperity and wise leadership.

In keeping with the prophecy of Samuel, these books also tell how the weaknesses of various kings led, first, to the division of the land into two kingdoms, Israel and Judah, and then to the total dissolution of both kingdoms. In 2 Kings, the nation of Assyria conquers the Israelites, and the citizens of Judah come to live as captives in Babylonia.

First Kings opens with David's death and Solomon's successful ascension to the throne. Having prayed for wisdom, Solomon significantly expands the kingdom, rebuilding its cities. Most important, it is he who constructs the great temple in Jerusalem to hold the Ark of the Covenant. Yet, because he allows his many foreign-born wives to worship their own gods, Solomon himself eventually turns away from God. This so angers God that He induces the northern tribes to revolt, splitting the kingdom in half. The ten northern tribes form the Kingdom of Israel, and the tribes of Judah and Benjamin come to make up the Kingdom of Judah.

Besides detailing the rich histories of the many kings who ruled the two kingdoms, 1 and 2 Kings also feature the prophets Elijah and Elisha. Elijah first appears as he attempts to resurrect monotheism for a people who have forgotten their covenant. (Even Ahab, the king of Israel at the time, was a Baal worshiper.) By putting the prophets of Baal to death, Elijah earns the enmity of Ahab's wife, Jezebel. After God takes Elijah up to heaven in a whirlwind, his successor, Elisha, is responsible for delivering God's message to an unfaithful people. Yet, by the time Elisha dies, Israel is overrun by Assyrians, who exile the Hebrew tribes and bring in their own idols.

Though there are righteous kings, such as Josiah, who find the Books of Law and renew the covenant with the Lord, 2 Kings ends with the destruction of the Temple of Solomon and his people's return to captivity.

The Miracle at the Grave of Elisha

Life of Solomon

SOLOMON RULES ISRAEL JUSTLY, IMPRESSING OTHERS WITH HIS WISDOM.
DISTRACTED BY HIS WEALTH, HE ALLOWS HIS WIVES TO WORSHIP OTHER GODS,
COMPELLING THE LORD TO DIVIDE ISRAEL AFTER HIS DEATH.

Solomon, son of David, ushered in Israel's golden age. Anointed king over his older brother, Adonijah, Solomon settles David's final conflicts and executes Adonijah in order to secure his position.

Solomon's reign gleams with promise when he is still very young; he dreams that God offers to give him anything he wants. Solomon's sole request is for wisdom—that he may rule his people with justice. God is so pleased that He not only promises Solomon wisdom but also grants him something he has not asked for: more wealth and honor than any other king.

Solomon's knowledge impresses not only his own people—kings of other nations also send their emissaries to hear him. The Queen of Sheba travels all the way from Ethiopia for a consultation. When two women go before Solomon with a child each claims as her own, he orders the child cut in two. When one of the women objects and insists the other one take the child instead, Solomon rules the true mother is the one who

King Solomon receiving the Queen of Sheba

does not want the child hurt.

Solomon's universal respect and renown enables him to easily make pacts and trade agreements with neighboring nations. To ensure these agreements, he takes brides from many powerful foreign families, including the daughter of the Egyptian pharaoh. These alliances bring enormous prosperity to Israel, allowing Solomon to realize David's dream of building a temple to hold the Ark of the Covenant.

The Judgment of Solomon

And Solomon did evil in the sight of the Lord,
and went not fully after the Lord, as *did* David his father.

1 KINGS 11:6

The construction of this most important edifice in the nation of Israel, as well as the celebrations that mark its consecration, is detailed in 1 Kings.

Yet, as Solomon's wealth grows, he unfortunately allows his seven hundred wives and three hundred concubines to practice whatever religion they choose; he even builds an altar to the goddess Astarte. Enraged, God vows to take away his kingdom. As Solomon comes to favor the southern Judean tribes (where David originates), the northern peoples grow to resent him. Though God promises to keep Solomon's kingdom intact while he is living, upon Solomon's death God divides the kingdom and under his son, Rehoboam, the northern uprising succeeds.

SOLOMON'S TEMPLE

God allows Solomon to realize his father's dream of a great temple. Intended to hold the Ark of the Covenant, the temple took seven years to build. Workmen precisely crafted all its pieces before they were transported to the temple site.

KING DAVID originally purchased the current site of the Dome of the Rock for the construction of a temple. Scholars believe that this is also the location to which Abraham took Isaac for sacrifice.

In the Bible, David dreams of erecting a magnificent building worthy of the Ark of the Covenant. God forbids David from doing so, however, because he had shed blood in war. God instead selects Solomon, David's son, to complete the task.

Because no one in the Jewish state can design and build such an edifice, Solomon calls upon the Phoenician king, Hiram of Tyre, who had built several temples to his own gods. Solomon arranges for Hiram's master craftsmen to work alongside both Hebrew workers and enslaved, unskilled laborers.

The realization of Solomon's temple is detailed in 1 Kings 5–9 and 2 Chronicles 2–7—its design, execution, costs, and

Solomon's Temple

eventual consecration. It takes seven years to complete the temple and thirteen to finish the palace buildings: the House of the Forest of Lebanon, the Hall of Pillars, the Hall of the Throne, the Hall of Judgment,

and Solomon's living quarters. Solomon forces some 30,000 workers into labor to cut cedar and cypress in Lebanon, 70,000 men to quarry the stone foundation, and 3,300 foremen to oversee the progress. Because

So Solomon built the house, and finished it.
1 KINGS 6:14

the men carefully fashioned the stone and timber before bringing it to the site, "neither hammer nor axe nor any tool of iron heard in the house, while it was in building." (1 Kings 6:7).

Bronze features at the temple entrance included two columns, Jachin and Boaz, festooned with two hundred pomegranates surrounding each of the lily-shaped capitals, as well as a bronze altar for burnt offerings and a thirty-ton "molten sea," which held ten thousand gallons of water that the priests used for ritual cleansing. The Bible describes rare wood carved with cherubim, palms, and flowers, all covered in gold, as well as altars, lamps, and other furnishings.

At the dedication of the Temple, priests place the Ark containing the two stone tablets of the Ten Commandments in the inner sanctuary—the Holy of Holies—a cube-shaped chamber measuring about 35 feet on each side. Once a year, on the Day of Atonement, the faithful opened this sanctum sanctorum.

The Temple of Solomon stood for 360 years, until the Babylonians razed it in 587 BCE.

King Solomon beholds the Ark of the Covenant being brought to the Temple

View of Jerusalem with the Temple of Solomon

The Kings of Israel and Judea

JEROBOAM CHALLENGES KING SOLOMON FOR THE THRONE. AFTER THE KINGDOM OF ISRAEL FALLS, SOLOMON'S SON REHOBOAM ASSUMES THE ROLE OF KING OVER A FRAGMENTED TERRITORY UNTIL ITS EVENTUAL COLLAPSE.

In the Bible, the prophet Samuel tells how God feels rejected when the people request the leadership of a king. But instead of punishing them for this folly, God instructs Samuel to do as the people wish. With God's help, Samuel selects the first king, Saul, but because of Saul's disobedience, God appoints David the next monarch. After the death of Saul and his sons, David ascends to the kingship of both Israel and Judea—a job his son, Solomon, eventually inherits.

King Solomon builds up the nation of Israel, using

Jeroboam's sacrifice at Bethel

conscripted labor and levying heavy taxes. In northern Israel, he spies Jeroboam, an impressive youth, working extremely hard and makes him the head of the forced laborers. Jeroboam receives a prophecy: God, unhappy with Solomon, wants ten of the Twelve Tribes worship all over his country, and allows anyone to become a priest. Gradually, in both Judah and Israel, the people forget the covenant, considering the rulers of both kingdoms to be corrupt idol-worshipers who have abandoned the law. The northern kingdom lasts about

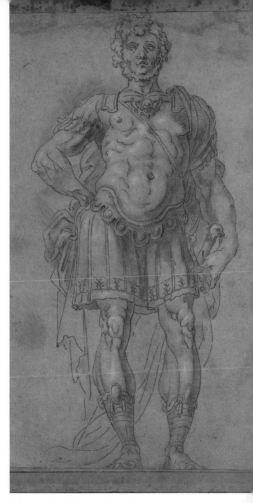

> And the man Jeroboam *was* a mighty man of valor: and Solomon seeing the young man that he was industrious, he made him ruler over all the charge of the house of Joseph.
>
> 1 KINGS 11:28

to form their own nation; he will make Jeroboam king if he agrees to follow God's laws. When Solomon hears, he tries to have Jeroboam killed, forcing Jeroboam to flee to Egypt.

Years later, when Solomon's son Rehoboam goes to Shechem in northern Israel to ascend the throne, the people ask him to reduce the heavy taxes imposed on them by his father. But instead of working reasonably with the people, Rehoboam increases their obligations under threats of dire punishment, ultimately forcing the northern tribes to form their own nation, installing Jeroboam as king.

Because Jeroboam does not want his people to travel to Jerusalem, home of the great temple, he builds places of

two hundred years, until Assyria defeats Israel in 721 BCE. Judah lasts scarcely three hundred before it, too, falls in 586 BCE— the great temple leveled and its inhabitants exiled to Babylonia.

A king of Judah and Israel

The destruction of the Temple at Jerusalem

Story of Elijah

FURIOUS ABOUT KING AHAB'S ACCEPTANCE OF THE DEMON BAAL, GOD PLAGUES ISRAEL WITH A DROUGHT. IT ENDS ONLY AFTER ELIJAH CHALLENGES BAAL'S PRIESTS TO A CONTEST AND PROVES VICTORIOUS.

After King Solomon, Israel suffers under the leadership of ill-suited kings for many generations. The worst of these is King Ahab. Not only does Ahab allow his wife, Jezebel of Sidon, to worship her god Baal, he builds altars to this foreign deity, as well. Elijah, a prophet wholly dedicated to the principle of the one God, confronts the king and predicts a three-year drought in Israel as punishment for this apostasy.

God bids Elijah to go into hiding near his home of Cherith. Ravens bring him food; he draws water from a brook until the predicted drought dries it up. God then directs Elijah to go to the town of Zarephath, where a poor widow awaits to help him. Though she is barely able to provide for herself and her son, she recognizes Elijah as a man of God and agrees to take him in. Miraculously, Elijah increases her food supply. When her son falls ill and dies, Elijah touches the boy and, with God's help, brings him back to life.

Three years into the drought, as it wreaks havoc on Israel,

> So Ahab went up to eat and to drink.
> And Elijah went up to the top of Carmel;
> and he cast himself down upon the earth,
> and put his face between his knees.
>
> 1 KINGS 18:42

Jezebel and Ahab

Elijah in the Wilderness

Elijah restoring the Widow's Son

God sends Elijah back to Ahab. Elijah conducts a contest on the top of Mount Carmel, where he decides to pit himself and his God against hundreds of priests faithful to Baal. Baal's priests invoke his name for an entire day with no result, yet when Elijah prays just once, God sends down a fire bolt. As rains come, ending the drought, the people rise up and kill all the priests of Baal.

Jezebel is enraged and vows vengeance on Elijah. He flees to Judah and walks forty days to Mount Sinai, becoming the first prophet to go there since Moses. Despairing, Elijah feels as if he is the only person left in Israel who is true to his God. The Lord whispers to him and orders him back to the world, where he picks Elijah's successor, Elisha. Elijah again shares a prophecy of demise with Ahab, badly frightening the king.

Elijah, whose name means "Yahweh is my God," never dies. On a journey to Bethel with Elisha, a chariot of fire claims him, pulling him up to heaven in a whirlwind. In his wake stands Elisha, the sole inheritor of his remarkable powers.

ASSYRIA AND BABYLONIA

Assyria and Babylonia were early empires in the fertile plain washed by the Tigris and Euphrates Rivers. They were both familiar with war and cruelty. Eventually, Isaiah's prophecy is fulfilled, and Cyrus II of Persia conquers Babylon.

IN ANCIENT TIMES, Assyria covered the area that now makes up the northern region of Iraq; Babylonia lay to the south. Both relied on the Euphrates and Tigris Rivers, whose water and silt deposits created a fertile alluvial plain. Clay tablets found near the original Sumerian settlement in the region date back five thousand years, and although the Sumerians knew how to craft metal into tools and armor

> Of a truth, Lord, the kings of Assyria have destroyed the nations and their lands.
>
> 2 KINGS 19:17

and practiced sophisticated war strategies, their history is a series of climaxes and declines.

Intricate Assyrian art showcases many battle scenes in gory detail. Assyria's cruelty and its methods of torture were well known and used as propaganda to instill fear in its enemies. Assyria was frequently at war with foreign powers, but in 627 BCE, rival kings dragged the nation into civil war, leaving it vulnerable to outside attack.

In the early 600s BCE, Babylonians joined forces with the Medes to conquer all of Assyria. Babylon then ruled Assyria until 539 BCE, leaving its cities in ruin and life intolerable.

Nimrod, grandson of Noah, founded Babylon. Assyria dominated Babylon from 911 BCE to 608 BCE. In 689 BCE, the Assyrians razed Babylon's walls, temples, and palaces, throwing the rubble into the sea. Under the reign of King Nebuchadnezzar, from 604 to 562 BCE, Babylonia rebuilt itself

Royal Lion Hunt

Scenes from the life of King Nebuchadnezzar

and became a wealthy city at the center of important trade routes. Babylon was renowned in the ancient world for its hanging gardens and double-wide city walls, which towered 203 feet high. Brickwork was glazed in yellow and red; gates were blue and decorated with reliefs of dragons, lions, and bulls; and the temples had golden domes.

Babylon was a world power at the time of Isaiah, hated for its destruction of Jerusalem and the Temple of Solomon in 587 BCE under King Nebuchadnezzar. Isaiah prophesied revenge—that God would open the fortified gates of Babylon to Cyrus II of Persia and his army (Isaiah 45:1). They would overthrow the kingdom (13:19) and the prideful city, in ruins, would become uninhabitable swampland—"I will sweep it with the besom of destruction, saith the Lord of hosts" (14:23). Cyrus conquered Babylon in 539 BCE, fulfilling Isaiah's prophecy. The city never again rose to power, gradually falling into decay.

Semiramis building Babylon

Josiah

ATTEMPTING TO RIGHT THE WRONGS DONE BY KINGS BEFORE HIM, JOSIAH IMPLEMENTS THE LAW OF MOSES IN ISRAEL. STILL, GOD IS ANGRY, AND, AFTER JOSIAH'S DEATH IN BATTLE, HIS PEOPLE LOSE THEIR PROMISED LAND.

Within three hundred years of Solomon's reign, Manasseh comes to rule Judah, the southern kingdom. He allows pagan religious practice, and, under his leadership, the people completely turn away from the God of Israel. Manasseh transforms Solomon's great temple into a place of Baal worship, building altars to pagan gods and goddesses. People make sacrifices to these gods throughout the land, and they ignore the Law of Moses.

God is furious—particularly over the desecration of His temple—and vows that Judah's inhabitants will suffer an even worse fate than their northern counterparts in Israel. After Manasseh dies, his son, Amon, becomes king. Amon continues in his father's footsteps until he is assassinated. His eight-year-old son, Josiah, then ascends the throne.

In the eighteenth year of King Josiah's reign, he commands the great temple in Jerusalem to be cleaned and renovated. While this work is being done, a high priest discovers a scroll and brings it to the king. Reading

Josiah destroys the Idols

> Behold therefore, I will gather thee unto thy fathers, and thou shalt be gathered into thy grave in peace; and thine eyes shall not see all the evil which I will bring upon this place.
>
> 2 KINGS 22:20

Josiah is made King

it, Josiah is horrified: these are the discarded Laws of Moses, which generations of kings have ignored. Josiah realizes how angry God is with his people when Uldah, a prophetess, warns him. Though God is aware of Josiah's repentance and will not wreak vengeance on Judah in his lifetime, He will nevertheless horribly punish the land in later years.

Josiah reads the laws to his people and all the high officials from the steps of the temple. He

Josiah brings back the feast of Passover

> And the king commanded all the people, saying, Keep the passover unto the Lord your God, as it is written in the book of this covenant.
>
> 2 KINGS 23:21

orders the destruction of every symbol of pagan worship. He mandates the removal from the temple and burning of artifacts dedicated to foreign gods and goddesses. Josiah goes on to desecrate and demolish altars built for sacrifices throughout the country, including those that Solomon himself erected for his wives. Josiah drives out fortune-tellers, mediums, and seers from the land. Most important of all, he resurrects and reinstates the feast of Passover, which has not been celebrated since the time of the judges.

Even though Judah has never seen a king so intent on obeying the Law of Moses, God remains angry with His people. Upon Josiah's death in battle, the four heirs to the throne are helpless to stave off a Babylonian invasion and the destruction of Solomon's temple. The Babylonians eject God's people from the Promised Land and force them into captivity.

The destruction of the Temple of Jerusalem

THE FIRST AND SECOND BOOKS OF
CHRONICLES

FOCUSING ON THE RULERS RESPONSIBLE FOR SIGNIFICANT RELIGIOUS REFORMATIONS—THE "GOOD" KINGS OF THE BIBLE—BOTH 1 CHRONICLES AND 2 CHRONICLES HIGHLIGHT AN EVOLVING RELIGIOUS COMMUNITY, WHILE RECOUNTING THE BOOKS THAT CAME BEFORE.

Like Kings and Samuel before them, the thirteenth and fourteenth books of the Bible were originally one document. While Chronicles reiterates the history contained in the previous two books, the perspective is that of a growing religious community. The origins and organization of spiritual worship

Slaughter of the sons of Zedekiah before their father

receive great emphasis, as does the genealogy of the Twelve Tribes of Israel. Written by exiled Babylonians, 1 and 2 Chronicles are primarily concerned with the history of Judah and its kings, all ancestors of King David. (Not having followed God's word, the Northern Kingdom of Israel, the writers believed, was not worthy of mention.)

First Chronicles begins with an accounting of the genealogy of the Israelites, starting with Adam. The main focus of 1 Chronicles is on King David and his greatness. Diverging from the portrait of David painted in earlier books, 1 Chronicles stresses the positive side of his nature. This book relates the conquest of Jerusalem and the moving of the Ark of the Covenant, as well as David's work designing and collecting materials and building a temple for the Ark. First Chronicles ends with the elevation of Solomon.

Second Chronicles features the achievements of King Solomon, describing the building and dedication of the great temple his father designed, and the arrival of the Ark of the

David's Victory

Covenant. After Solomon's death, the northern tribes split away and the Levite priests move to Judah, the result of Israel's improper way of worshiping. Unlike Kings, 2 Chronicles chooses to concentrate on the "good" kings—that is, those who enacted religious reforms during their reigns. The Bible credits Hezekiah with a great resurrection of faith and devotion, and mentions his instrumental role in his grandson Josiah's covenant with the Lord.

Jerusalem falls under its last king, Zedekiah. Its residents have mocked and ignored the warnings of God's prophets, importuning them to reform, and the Babylonian army destroys the city, enslaving its inhabitants. As prophesied by Jeremiah, the land lies desolate for seventy years.

Second Chronicles concludes as Cyrus II, the emperor of Persia, having conquered Babylon, orders the return of the Israelites to Jerusalem.

Return from Exile

ONCE THE BABYLONIAN EMPIRE FALLS, THE ISRAELITES RETURN TO THEIR PROMISED LAND. ISRAEL IS IN SHAMBLES BUT THE PEOPLE PERSEVERE, RECONSTRUCTING SOLOMON'S TEMPLE AND JERUSALEM'S CITY WALLS.

Some 48 years after it had wreaked the catastrophic destruction of Jerusalem, the Babylonian Empire fell to the armies of Cyrus II of Persia. Also known as Cyrus the Great, the Persian emperor ordered the Israelites to return to their land in Judah and rebuild their city and their temple.

In 539 BCE, although many Israelites have settled happily in Babylon, a priest named Zerubbabel heeds the command of Cyrus and leads the return of the first group of several thousand exiles. Many are Levite priests, but the majority of these settlers come from the tribes of Benjamin and Judah.

On arriving at their old city, the exiles find an inhospitable wasteland, so they immediately set to work rebuilding the temple foundations. While some shout in joy, the few priests who remember the splendor of Solomon's building, which housed the now-lost Ark of the Covenant, cry bitterly.

The Samaritans living on the land offer to help. Though many of the Samaritans are ancestors of the northern Tribes of Israel and consider themselves to be of the same faith, Zerubbabel, recalling the different ways they practice their religion, rejects them. Work on the temple stops for the next 18 years as hostilities ensue.

The Israelites, though significantly demoralized, finally manage to complete their temple in 516 BCE. About sixty years later, Ezra, who is devoted to propagating the Laws

Emperor Cyrus the Great of Persia

The Jews return to Jerusalem in the time of Cyrus

of Moses, leads a much larger group out of exile. It is after their return that the Israelites first refer to themselves as "Jews"—the word deriving from both the tribe of Judah and the inhabitants of the land of Judah. The Jews now identify themselves by their clans, not their tribes. The Samaritans,

Ezra reads the Law to the People

endure tense relations with their Jewish neighbors into the time of the New Testament.

city enables the inhabitants to live there safely. As governor, Nehemiah also moves one tenth

---

Thus saith Cyrus king of Persia, The Lord God of heaven hath given me all the kingdoms of the earth; and he hath charged me to build him an house at Jerusalem, which *is* in Judah.

EZRA 1:2

---

who the Jews consider impure in blood as a result of intermarriage (and in religious practice, because they worship idols at their own altars),

Some 12 years after Ezra settles in Jerusalem, Nehemiah arrives; he rebuilds the walls of the city of Jerusalem in 52 days. The fortification of the

of those living in the surrounding cities in Judah into Jerusalem, securing its place as the center of Jewish life for the next two hundred years.

EZRA

FOLLOWING THE PROCLAMATION OF PREVIOUS EMPERORS,
EZRA HELPS LEAD A SECOND GROUP OF EXILES BACK TO JERUSALEM.
HE TAKES IT AS HIS DUTY TO PURIFY THE ISRAELITES' BLOODLINES SO
THAT THEY CAN RIGHTFULLY RECLAIM THEIR PROMISED LAND.

The eponymous fifteenth book of the Bible, at one time combined with Nehemiah, begins with a third-person recounting of the Israelites' return to the Promised Land. It switches to a first-person account with Ezra's appearance halfway through the book. Some historians believe that Ezra wrote 1 and 2 Chronicles, as well as this book: both rely on official accounts and memoirs as sources.

Ezra opens with a proclamation from Cyrus the Great, the Persian emperor who has defeated and occupied Babylon. Moved by God, Cyrus orders the Israelites living in Babylon to return to Jerusalem and rebuild the temple destroyed by the Babylonians. A census follows, counting all of those who joined this first journey back to Jerusalem.

The returnees joyfully begin reconstructing Solomon's great temple. Yet, their happiness is short-lived. When they refuse to allow any of their former enemies to assimilate, they inspire much local opposition. Work on the temple stops for 18 years, only to resume when two prophets insist upon it. Darius, the new emperor of Persia and ally of the Jews, finds Cyrus's original proclamation and orders the work completed.

Many years later, Ezra, a new emperor—as well as a scholar and expert on Mosaic Law—leads a second wave of Israelites back to Jerusalem. His entourage consists of many Levite priests and temple workers. Here, the Book of Ezra switches to a first-person account, describing how Ezra encourages the Israelites to honor their temple. He voices how shocked he is to find that God's people, upon their return from exile, are no longer pure. Many of the Jewish men have, in fact, taken foreign wives, in direct opposition to the Law of Moses. It is up to Ezra to purify the race so that the Israelites may retain their possession of the Promised Land. He decides that these illicit marriages should dissolve; the foreign wives and the children from these unions must be sent away. The Book of Ezra concludes with a list of men who had married outside their faith, but now comply with Ezra's decree.

OPPOSITE PAGE: *Ezra kneels in Prayer*

THE BOOK OF
NEHEMIAH

THE BOOK OF NEHEMIAH MARKS THE FULL RETURN OF THE ISRAELITES
TO JERUSALEM. NEHEMIAH BECOMES GOVERNOR AND IMPOSES ORDER,
TRANSFORMING JERUSALEM INTO A FLOURISHING CITY.

If Ezra chronicles the priestly class's experience, Nehemiah depicts the work of a practical man of action. A companion to Ezra, the sixteenth book of the Bible details the exiles' eventual complete return to Jerusalem. In both books, each protagonist begins their journey only after spending time in rigorous prayer.

Nehemiah is a pious man with a prestigious job—he is the emperor's wine steward in Babylon—who is greatly upset to see the returnees to Jerusalem fare poorly. He knows the misery of the few Israelites who managed to escape exile. The surrounding foreigners look down upon God's people, though they are back in their Promised Land. The

Nehemiah viewing secretly the ruins of the walls of Jerusalem

walls of Jerusalem remain in ruins. Seeing Nehemiah's sadness, Emperor Artaxerxes sends him into Judah accompanied by an official escort. Within days, Nehemiah organizes the Israelites into construction crews who begin to rebuild the walls and gates of Jerusalem. Mocked by three local men for attempting this seemingly impossible task and threatened by neighboring townsmen, Nehemiah and his crew nevertheless continue to work—tools in one hand, weapons in the other. They complete their task in just 52 days.

Nehemiah's official connections and superb leadership skills result in his appointment as governor. Citing the great disparities in wealth among Israelites, he orders all debts cancelled in order to free the poor from the crushing loans that they owe their brethren. Nehemiah himself refuses the gold and silver tributes usually paid to the governor. Ezra reads the Law of

Returning to Jerusalem several years later, Nehemiah is appalled to find the temple misused, the Sabbath not universally observed, and many

Nehemiah, the King's Cupbearer

But the former governors that *had been* before me were chargeable unto the people, and had taken of them bread and wine, beside forty shekels of silver; yea, even their servants bare rule over the people: but so did not I, because of the fear of God.

NEHEMIAH 5:15

Moses to the people. Realizing how far they have strayed, they vow to be more loyal to God than were their ancestors, who were punished for their sins.

After 12 years, Nehemiah journeys to Babylon to report to the emperor.

Jewish men failing to keep their bloodlines pure. Nehemiah corrects these sacrileges and enforces order and regulation in worship. With the temple, walls, and gate completed, Jerusalem is, once again, a thriving city.

THE BOOK OF
ESTHER

THE BOOK OF ESTHER NEVER MENTIONS GOD'S NAME, THOUGH HE REMAINS A SILENT, PROTECTIVE PRESENCE. FAVORED BY THE EMPEROR OF PERSIA, ESTHER'S COURAGE INSPIRES THE JEWISH PEOPLE TO DEFEND THEMSELVES.

Ahasuerus makes Esther queen

The setting of Esther is the vastness of the Persian Empire, stretching from India to Ethiopia. The only book of the Bible that does not mention God's name, Esther takes place at the winter palace of Emperor Ahasuerus around the same time as Ezra.

When the emperor's wife disobeys him while he is hosting a banquet, his advisers decide that, should this foul deed go unpunished, the women of Persia will likewise disobey their husbands. They decree, as a result, that there will be a new queen. Ahasuerus summons the most beautiful virgins in the country to the capital—among them is a Jewish orphan named Esther.

Of all the young women he meets, Esther is the one the most appealing to Ahasuerus though he has no idea that she is Jewish. He makes her his queen and appoints Mordecai, her cousin and guardian, to an administrative post. Upon learning of a plot to kill the emperor, Mordecai stops it, and a royal secretary makes official note of his allegiance.

Haman, the prime minister, does not see Mordecai in the same favorable light. Upon learning that Mordecai

is a Jew, Haman forces the emperor to sign an edict calling for the killing of all Jews in the kingdom, throwing lots to decide the day of the pogrom. Mordecai induces Esther to approach the emperor in his inner sanctum, an offense punishable by death. She does this willingly, to save her people, and amazingly escapes punishment. When Esther invites Ahasuerus and Haman to a banquet, Mordecai again offends Haman, who builds a gallows to hang Mordecai. Awoken by construction noise, Ahasuerus reads the public record and discovers how Mordecai saved his life. He calls for a public tribute to Mordecai, further infuriating Haman. When Esther informs the emperor that she and Mordecai will

be among the victims of the pogrom, Ahasuerus sentences Haman to be hanged in his own gallows. He allows Esther to write a proclamation, in which she orders Jews to defend themselves against the forthcoming violence. When the day of the pogrom arrives, the Jews destroy their enemies throughout the kingdom, an event subsequently commemorated by the Feast of Purim.

Esther before Ahasuerus

Go, gather together all the Jews . . . and fast ye for me, and neither eat nor drink three days, night or day: I also and my maidens will fast likewise; . . . and if I perish, I perish.

ESTHER 4:16

The Triumph of Mordecai

The
Wisdom Books

While the Pentateuch and the Historical Books are narratives that tell stories of the creation of the world and the history of the Jewish people, the Wisdom Books, in contrast, offer dialogues, poems, musings, and songs. Each of the five—from the Book of Job to the 150 songs of Psalms, from insightful Proverbs to cynical Ecclesiastes, ending with the joyful Song of Solomon—explores a different existential struggle and asks questions about God's relationship with the individual.

Job's story, for example, poses the often-heard moral question, "Why do bad things happen to good people?" Psalms, which range from songs of praise to cries for help, spans the range of human emotion, and the folk wisdom of Proverbs provides insight into wise living, with commonsense epigrams dispensing advice on such topics as honesty, humility, hard work, and civility. Written from the point of view of a man who has everything, the mordant, fatalistic Ecclesiastes acknowledges that we are all truly doomed to die, yet, in what can hardly be a more visceral contrast, we have the Song of Solomon—a set of poems that celebrate love and sexuality and extol the joys of nature—to conclude the Wisdom Books.

Song of Songs

THE BOOK OF
JOB

JOB, ONE OF THE BIBLE'S MOST PIOUS MEN, ENDURES A SERIES OF UNBELIEVABLE TESTS AT THE HANDS OF GOD. THOUGH HE QUESTIONS GOD'S PLAN, HE MAINTAINS HIS FAITH, AND GOD REWARDS HIS SUFFERING.

Job, the first of the Wisdom books and the eighteenth book of the Bible, presents the story of a good man afflicted with every conceivable kind of bad luck. Job, using sarcasm, wit, and anger, debates his three friends about his sudden turn of fortune. They seek to discover why an all-powerful God would punish such a pious believer, while many unprincipled men prosper. Ultimately, God himself settles their argument.

In a prologue, God discusses Job's virtues and loyalty with Satan, his adversary. Job is a wealthy man living in Uz; he has property, flocks of sheep and cattle, a wife and ten children,

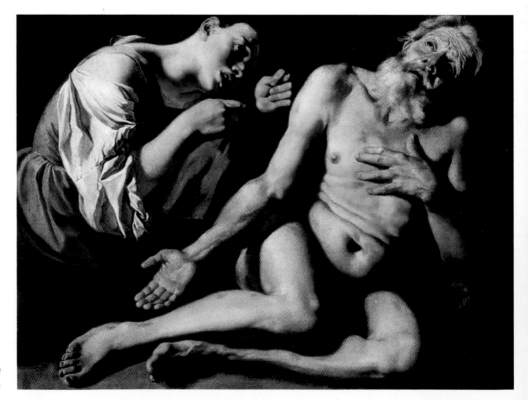

Job mocked by his wife

Job and his False Comforters

his skin, penniless, and reduced to ruin. Three friends join Job in his mourning. Job speaks on the seventh day, wondering why God has allowed such horrible things to befall him and cursing the day he was born. Each friend suggests that Job has obviously not atoned for sins he has committed, perhaps secretly. Job, denying this, desires a confrontation with God. A fourth man joins them; he points out the necessity of suffering in order to appreciate what one has. When he, too, suggests Job's suffering is his own fault, God, speaking from a whirlwind, interrupts the debate. Warning the men not to question when they know so little, God evokes all the great and mysterious things He does, and Job is overwhelmed by God's unlimited power.

Restored to health, Job finds himself twice as wealthy as he was before, surrounded by a new family in the end.

and enjoys perfect health, as well as the respect of his community. He is also a faithful man of God. When Satan points out that it is easy to be virtuous when one is so surrounded by ample

> There was a man in the land of Uz, whose name *was* Job; and that man was perfect and upright, and one that feared God, and eschewed evil.
>
> JOB 1:1

rewards, God allows Satan to test Job in whatever way he sees fit, short of killing him. In the course of a single day, Satan kills Job's children and takes all his possessions. Job mourns, bemoaning his fate, but he does not curse God. The next day Satan covers Job in sores. Job sits on the outskirts of town, scraping

Job restored to prosperity

THE BOOK OF
PSALMS

SACRED TO CHRISTIANS AND JEWS ALIKE, THE PSALMS ARE POEMS AND SONGS THAT REMIND THE FAITHFUL OF THE GREATNESS OF GOD, THE POWER OF FAITH AND FORGIVENESS, AND THE BLESSINGS OF HUMAN LIFE.

The word *psalm* derives from the Greek *psalmos*, meaning "song." The nineteenth book of the Bible is a collection of 150 sacred songs and poems, called "psalms." Often used in religious services, the Book of Psalms provides great inspiration to both Christians and Jews. Whether used during private prayers, in public

Marble panel showing children singing and playing music to illustrate Psalm 150

Psalm 68: "Let God arise, let his enemies be scattered"

worship, or at a site of pilgrimage, it demonstrates the necessity of trusting God completely and looking to Him as both protector and refuge from the iniquities of humanity.

According to tradition, King David was the primary writer of Psalms, but the range of subjects and historical references strongly suggests that there were other contributors as well.

Divided into five sections, the work deals with such issues as God's power and His relationship with humankind.

Jerusalem, referred to in the text as "Zion," is the place most often mentioned in Psalms as the dwelling place of the Lord. Many deal with the resurrection of Jerusalem and assert the future global prominence of that city. Composed largely during a time of exile, Psalms expresses the pain of a people separated from a homeland and stresses the importance of the Promised Land to future generations of Jews. For Christians praising or giving thanks to God, many psalms detail His endless accomplishments and hail His awesome power.

There are also historic psalms, which stress God's special relationship

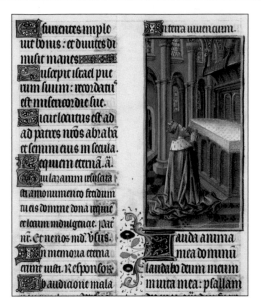

Psalm 145: "I will extol thee, my God, O king"

and are timeless in their relevance. Still other psalms beg forgiveness, demand vengeance, or celebrate festivities and religious holidays.

> God is our refuge and strength, a very present help in trouble. Therefore will not we fear, though the earth be removed, and though the mountains be carried into the midst of the sea.
>
> PSALM 46:1–2

with the Jewish people. Many of these passages are devoted to the Law of Moses, with individual prayers listing these laws, expressing confidence in them, and emphasizing the importance of obedience. Others, which lament or invoke help for those in despair or suffering from physical affliction, mirror the human condition

Among all the books in the Old Testament, the ancient Hebrew poems of Psalms best convey the universal need for faith in God. Playing a fundamental role in Christian worship, Psalms underlines the limitless power of God and portends the coming Messiah, who frequently quotes from Psalms in His teachings.

MUSIC IN THE BIBLE

Music and lyrical language hold special places in the Bible, especially in the Book of Psalms. The earliest songs preserved culture and history, forming bridges between disparate communities to join them in praise of one god.

BEFORE DAVID himself became king, he was a musician, brought to the palace to soothe King Saul's tormented soul by playing the harp.

Music flourished during David's reign. He commissioned hymns and psalms and invited skilled Phoenician musicians into his kingdom in an effort to

The Song of Miriam

King David playing the harp

elevate the Israelites' primitive forms of music. Historians credit him with writing 73 of the 150 psalms. In addition to their universal subject matter, the psalms draw upon musical and poetic traditions of neighboring lands; three thousand years later, they are still beloved.

Music featured in the Feast of the Tabernacles, which included dancing, burning torches, and Levites chanting psalms to the melodies of flutes. The prophets also used music: skilled musicians induced a trancelike state in their listeners as the prophets called upon the power of God.

In instrumental music, stringed instruments (the harp, lyre, and lute) and percussion instruments (timbrel, frame drum, cymbals,

> Praise him with the sound of the trumpet: praise him with the psaltery and harp. Praise him with the timbrel and dance: praise him with stringed instruments and organs. Praise him upon the loud cymbals.
>
> PSALM 150:3–5

various shakers, and rhythm bones) dominated, as did wind instruments, such as the silver trumpet, shofar (ram's horn), reed pipe, and flute. The blast of the shofar announced the anointing of a king and the beginning of a feast day. In combat, it marked orders to break camp and mobilize, a battle charge, a battle victory, or God's impending judgment.

In a preliterate society, vocal music was an attractive medium for conveying society's history, laws, and traditions, which were easier to remember if sung, typically accompanied by a lyre. For funerals, the reed pipe (a cousin of today's oboe) approximated the wailing of mourners.

Saint John the Divine's visions of the end times in the Book of Revelation include songs sung by mystical beasts and elders, songs of praise to God the father and His Son, songs of God's triumph over the enemies of His people, and songs of the defeat of the unfaithful city

The Seven Trumpets

and persecutor of saints. It is the sound of seven trumpets sounded by seven angels that will herald the Apocalypse. In Revelation 18:22, after the mighty angel of the Lord tears down Babylon, the music stops: "And the voice of harpers, and musicians, and of pipers, and trumpeters, shall be heard no more at all in thee."

Shofar, a ram's-horn wind instrument

THE BOOK OF
PROVERBS

IN CONTRAST WITH THE INTENSITY OF PSALMS AND THE GRAVITY OF ECCLESIASTES, THE BOOK OF PROVERBS IMPARTS SUCCINCT, MEMORABLE ADVICE ON WISDOM, MORALITY, AND EVERYDAY LIVING.

A proverb is a short, well-known saying that expresses an obvious truth and generally offers advice. The twentieth book of the Bible is deceptively simple and enjoyable in

its composition, yet its main theme, stressed again and again, is the importance of living with wisdom.

King Solomon, regarded by many as the primary writer of this book,

Illustration to Proverbs 11:26

.DI. ☉ .H.
DIE SPRICH SALOMO DAS XI CAPITEL
WER KORN INHELT DEM FLVCHEN DIE LEIT
ABER SEGEN KOMPT VBER DEN SO ES VERKAFFT
M D XXXIIII

> Train up a child in the way he should go: and when he is old, he will not depart from it.
>
> PROVERBS 22:6

was famous across the land for originating three thousand proverbs. The Book of Proverbs dispenses advice on topics large and small, ranging from simple common sense and good manners to much weightier matters of religious morality.

The first nine chapters of Proverbs consist of short stories and essays praising wisdom and comparing it to stupidity. The proverbs warn against laziness, debt, adultery, and immorality. Solomon's proverbs follow, making up an extensive portion of the book. They are written in short comparative sentences, for example, Proverbs 14:15: "The simple believeth every word: but the prudent man looketh well to his going." The proverbs often compare the difference in behavior between the foolish person and the wise. Fools lack not only morality but also any sense of self-awareness, nor are they interested in correcting their behavior. Indeed, a person reading these ancient proverbs today can easily recognize many modern archetypes in their short, pithy statements.

Proverbs especially honors the wisdom of women, particularly mothers, and numerous sayings and stories exemplify the handing down of advice and knowledge from parents to children.

The Judgment of Solomon

The aim of Proverbs is to influence humanity's will by offering practical advice for people at every stage of life. While the Psalms are emotional appeals to God, and Ecclesiastes is written from a cerebral viewpoint, Proverbs seeks to shape the reader's behavior and actions, and one need not be highly educated or intellectual to understand these short, clever messages that cut to the quick. The sayings in Proverbs impart practical guidance for everyday civility, enjoin the faithful to maintain a functioning community, and warn them against the immoral and stubborn individuals who will never change.

Near the end of Proverbs are the Words of Agur, also credited to Solomon. They essentially serve as a reminder that—after all these sensible words of wisdom—one is helpless if not with God.

MARRIAGE, FAMILY, AND SOCIETY

The Old Testament assigns particular value to the commitment of marriage.
Not only a bond between a man and a woman, marriage also shapes
the family structure and provides for the proper rearing of children.

IN BIBLICAL TIMES, parents arranged marriages for their children. Instead of dating and courtship prior to marriage, the future husband and wife, with their families, negotiated a betrothal, or binding agreement, resulting in marriage. This agreement, once reached, was irrevocable—only divorce could break it. Families arranged most marriages by the time their daughters reached just 12 or 13 years of age.

In the Bible, people practiced polygamy, though only wealthy men could afford to have numerous wives. Society also permitted concubines, especially in cases where a husband's wife could not produce children. Generally, men took concubines during times of war, or from the lower classes.

It was customary for a girl to work at home, so the groom's parents had to pay

Marriage at Cana

compensation to her family when she married and moved to her husband's house. Marriages were not sanctioned civically or religiously, and there was no official ceremony; rather, communities celebrated the agreement with a procession and a feast, after which the bride joined her husband's household.

The marriage was then subject to many religious rules.

The law bound a woman to her husband, for example, so long as he lived; only his death released her from this obligation. Wives were to take care of the house and the needs of the family, never usurping the primacy of the husband. Husbands were to provide for their families, leaving an inheritance to their grandchildren. A child's birthright derived not from the mother, but from the father, and male children had superior property rights.

A man was expected to marry his brother's childless widow. Mores forbade intermarriage with foreigners; most people married within their own tribe.

In the Old Testament, divorce was granted on any grounds, freeing both parties to remarry, while in the New Testament, Jesus stipulates that divorce should only be granted in cases of adultery.

The Bible stresses the critical importance of children honoring and obeying their parents, not only for the sake of preserving the family unit but also for strengthening the community; children who lack respect for their parents will have none for others. The patriarch is the head of the family, responsible for the religious direction of the entire household.

Jacob Blessing the Children of Joseph

The Betrothal of the Virgin

THE BOOK OF
ECCLESIASTES

ECCLESIASTES, ONE OF THE BIBLE'S MOST SUBSTANTIVE BOOKS, GRAPPLES WITH SEVERAL OF LIFE'S MOST CHALLENGING QUESTIONS. AMID THE SENSELESSNESS OF LIFE, THOUGH, THESE WRITINGS ASK THE READER TO FIND FAITH IN GOD AND HIS COMMANDMENTS.

The word *ecclesiastes* means "preacher." In the twenty-first book of the Bible, we gain access to the rather mordant thoughts of the wisest, richest king of Jerusalem. The narrator calls himself "the son of David," so scholars often attribute Ecclesiastes to King Solomon.

A man who "has everything," the book's narrator, or preacher, attempts to answer the question, "What will bring us permanent happiness?" Having sampled everything life has to offer, he concludes that most pursuits are useless

Ecclesiastes

> I the Preacher was king over Israel in Jerusalem. And I gave my heart to seek and search out by wisdom concerning all *things* that are done under heaven: this sore travail hath God given to the sons of man to be exercised therewith.
>
> ECCLESIASTES 1:12–13

and futile: "All is vanity." In Ecclesiastes we learn how the preacher acquired his riches. Although, as he says, everyone tries to be rich, it is the laborer who

ECCLESIASTES 3:1–8

To every thing there is a season, and
    a time to every purpose under the
    heaven:

A time to be born, and a time to die; a time
    to plant, and a time to pluck up that
    which is planted;

A time to kill, and a time to heal; a time to
    break down, and a time to build up;

A time to weep, and a time to laugh; a time
    to mourn, and a time to dance;

A time to cast away stones, and a time
    to gather stones together; a time to
    embrace, and a time to refrain from
    embracing;

A time to get, and a time to lose; a time to
    keep, and a time to cast away;

A time to rend, and a time to sew; a time
    to keep silence, and a time to speak;

A time to love, and a time to hate; a time
    of war, and a time of peace.

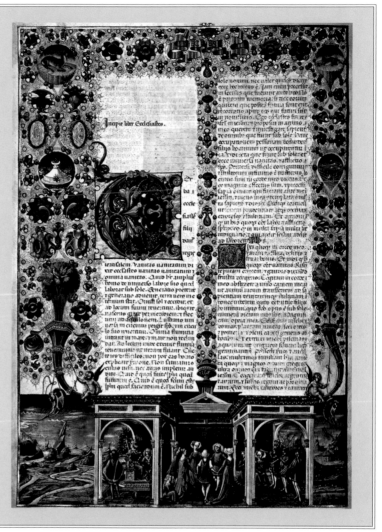

Illuminated manuscript of Ecclesiastes

sleeps well, for the more one attains, the more one must worry about retaining it. This wisdom has not made the preacher any happier. Nor, he says, are humans superior to any beast, for every living creature is destined for a grave. And although many imagine that they are creative, in reality, everything—the seasons and the endless cycle of human life—simply repeats over and over.

"There is nothing new under the sun," the teacher supposes.

After noting that the wicked frequently triumph over the good, and the innocent pay for the crimes of the guilty, Ecclesiastes ends with the injunction that we must always honor God's commandments, for God knows our deepest secrets and will be our ultimate judge.

THE SONG OF
SOLOMON

THE SONG OF SOLOMON STANDS OUT FOR ITS UNABASHED EXPRESSION OF EROTIC LOVE AND THE PLEASURES OF MONOGAMY. CHRISTIANS AND JEWS INTERPRET THE SONG AS A METAPHOR FOR ONE'S RELATIONSHIP WITH GOD.

The Song of Solomon celebrates love and pleasure

Readers frequently cite the twenty-second book of the Bible as the most beautiful. As lush and sensual as Ecclesiastes is dark and melancholic, the Song of Solomon celebrates all that is vibrant, fruitful, and pleasurable in the world. A series of love poems between a man and a woman, the book, also known as the Song of Songs or the Canticle of Canticles, also contains the thoughts of "the daughters of Jerusalem." One of the shortest books of the Bible, it consists of 117 verses; the name comes from the first line, "The song of songs, which is Solomon's."

In a series of six songs, the woman and man address each other, using imagery from nature that expresses great erotic desire. He compares her to a lily and a rose; she refers to him as a fruit tree. The first song describes the woman, darkly complexioned from working in the vineyards. The man praises her beauty and we follow their relationship—which takes place in gardens, vineyards, and wilderness—from courtship to consummation. The book similarly praises all manner of vegetation and animal life. Not since the Garden of Eden in Genesis has the Bible so joyfully celebrated nature, and this ardent, almost mystical expression of sexuality brings the lovers back to an idyllic state that recalls Eden.

Though attributed to King Solomon, Song of Songs may have been written by others in his honor. At one point, the woman declares that she sees the king carried on his throne, and the man voices his complete satisfaction with

The Song of Songs: the Shulammite Maiden

one vineyard, compared to Solomon's many. Some consider this observation a veiled rebuke of Solomon (for his seven hundred wives and three hundred concubines), promoting the joys of monogamy over sexual profligacy.

The Song of Solomon does not invoke God's name, but Jewish scholars nevertheless consider it a sacred text because it serves as an allegory of God's relationship with His people. The woman—the object of the man's desire—represents the Jewish people, while the man represents God, ardor, and devotion. Similarly, Christians view this book of the Bible as a metaphor epitomizing Christ's relationship with the church, and the soul's relationship with God.

The Song of Songs is an allegory of God's relationship with his people

LOVE AND SEXUALITY

The Bible largely considers romance and sexual relations a means
to reproducing within a monogamous union. Some sections celebrate
the sensuality of life, but the focus remains on God.

JACOB—SO ENAMORED of
Rachel that he agrees to work
for her father for seven years in
order to win her hand—is one
of the relatively few cases of
romantic love portrayed in the
Bible. Though nothing surpasses
the Song of Solomon in its
celebration of the joys of erotic

Levite and his concubine at Gibeah

*The Fiancée of the Night from
the Song of Solomon*

and romantic love, and Proverbs
is full of wise words on love and
marriage, romance in the Bible is
less a priority than it is an honor
and responsibility.

God commands Adam
and Eve to "Be fruitful, and
multiply" (Genesis 1:28), and
yet the first record of biblical
intercourse occurs only after
the two of them have left the
Garden of Eden. Survival, of
course, depends on continually

increasing the numbers of the
Hebrew tribal populations;
accordingly, the people
eventually come to accept
the practices of polygamy and
concubinage.

Deuteronomy, however, lays
down stringent rules for the
proper observance of sexual
relations. Sex is allowed between
a man and a woman within
marriage, and it is generally
forbidden when it does not lead

to conception—considered an affront to God's directive to multiply. When a woman is menstruating, sex is forbidden; there is to be a seven-day cleanse before relations may resume.

Many interpretations of the Bible conclude that homosexuality and bestiality are abominations. Though intermarriage between cousins within families is common, incest is forbidden.

Adultery, as laid out in the Ten Commandments, goes against the Law of God, and the New Testament goes so far as to consider the act of lusting after another's spouse a form of adultery. A husband must love his wife and should regularly have intercourse with her in order to avoid infidelity (Proverbs 5:18–19). A man is not to leave his wife for the first year of marriage to go off to

battle but is, rather, enjoined to stay with her to "cheer her up."

A raped woman can only prove her innocence if a witness hears her cry out for help—if no witness comes forward, then the law considers her equally guilty of the crime. If a man rapes a virgin who is betrothed to another, he is to be put to death; if she is unattached, he must pay her father and marry her—a question of property rights.

Jacob encountering Rachel with her father's herds

The Prophets

Many of the Bible's books contain scattered prophetic text, but Prophets, the final section of the Old Testament, focuses on the writings of those who God inspired to advocate for Him during the three hundred years linking the rise, fall, and rebuilding of the nation of Israel.

God chose the prophets for their mission because of their evolved spirituality. No prophet ever sought the position—nor did many people respect him for taking it. The prophets' viewpoints reflected their diverse backgrounds, yet their mission was the same: to reform the people by reminding them of their covenant with God. Using writings, visions, dreams, symbolic actions, and preaching, they warned of coming chastisement, hoping the people would change course, offering hope for a distant future when warnings went unheeded and divine wrath seemed inescapable. Christians find evidence of the Messiah's coming in the prophetic books, and the New Testament frequently quotes Isaiah, Micah, Zechariah, and Malachi in this regard.

Ezekiel is a prophet

THE BOOK OF
ISAIAH

ISAIAH, THE FIRST BOOK OF THE SECTION OF THE BIBLE KNOWN AS THE PROPHETS, FIRST CONDEMNS THE ISRAELITES FOR THEIR WAYWARDNESS BEFORE OFFERING HOPE FOR A BRIGHTER FUTURE.

Isaiah is one of the greatest prophets in the Old Testament. His name, symbolic of his message, literally translates as "the Lord is salvation," and the Book of Isaiah is sometimes referred to as "the book of salvation."

Written in the politically turbulent years between 740 BCE and 680 BCE, Isaiah's prophecies were directed mainly at those living in Jerusalem and the Kingdom of Judah. Warning his contemporaries that their lack of faith will result in punishment from God, Isaiah is also credited with prophesying beyond his own life span: he foretells the future destruction of Jerusalem by Babylon, as well as the rise of Cyrus the Great of Persia and the release of the Jewish people from exile.

The second part of Isaiah foresees the rebirth of Jerusalem as a religious haven

Prophet Isaiah is an important prophet in both the Old and New Testament

Also I heard the voice of the Lord, saying, Whom shall I send, and who will go for us? Then said I, Here am I; send me.

ISAIAH 6:8

for people from every corner of the earth. Christians, as a result of Isaiah's prediction of the coming of a king with the bloodlines of David, consider Isaiah an extremely important book of the Bible, and it is widely quoted by the New Testament writers.

When King Ahaz opts to put his nation under the protection of Assyria to protect the people from the alliance of Syria and Israel, Isaiah advises him to turn instead to God for protection. He rightly predicts the Northern Kingdom of Israel will be completely overrun and destroyed by Assyria. Though Isaiah's people of the Southern Kingdom of Judah fear the same fate, Isaiah insists that they look for protection to none other but God. King Hezekiah ultimately agrees to follow this advice, and as a menacing Assyrian force gathers outside the gates of Jerusalem, God

King Uzziah stricken with leprosy

Isaiah is one of the later prophets

Isaiah was related to one of the kings of Judah, and he enjoyed a privileged position in society, with free access to the royalty of his day. His visions and predictions span the reigns of four kings—Uzziah, Jotham, Ahaz, and Hezekiah.

The book opens at a time when God is greatly dissatisfied with His people in Jerusalem, who enjoy many luxuries, while making only token motions of religious observance. Yet, for the poor, the courts offer no justice, and no one is looking out for those in a lower station of life. When Isaiah hears the Lord calling him to be a prophet, in the last year of King Uzziah's reign, he readily accepts, and from that moment on he becomes God's messenger, issuing warnings that are, alas, scarcely heeded.

strikes 185,000 troops dead in their campsites, and the Assyrians withdraw, retreating to their capital of Ninevah. When King Hezekiah falls ill, gift-bearing messengers visit him from Babylon. Isaiah questions Hezekiah; what did he show the Babylonians when he gave them a tour of his palace? Hezekiah answers that he showed them "everything." Isaiah then makes the

O Lord, be gracious unto us;
we have waited for thee:
be thou their arm every
morning, our salvation
also in the time of trouble.

ISAIAH 33:2

King Hezekiah

*Isaiah's Vision of the
Destruction of Babylon*

WHAT IS A PROPHET?

In the Bible, a prophet is far more than a person who can see into the future. Although, certainly, prophets did foretell of events yet to come, their purpose was to speak directly to the people on God's behalf, revealing His nature and His plans for His people, as explained in Deuteronomy 18:18: "I will raise them up a Prophet from among their brethren, like unto thee, and will put my words in his mouth; and he shall speak unto them all that I shall command him." Prophets not only foretold the future, they also issued warnings to those who had strayed or exhorted the faithful to worship with sincerity. For believers, the prophets were models of holiness, setting the standards for spiritual and ethical development. For others, they are figures of scorn.

Many biblical scholars assert that all later prophecy was an extension of the prophecy of Moses, the greatest of the prophets, to whom God had shown everything. Including Moses, the Old Testament lists 55 prophets: 48 men and 7 women. The Bible also includes a warning against false prophets: "But the prophet, which shall presume to speak a word in my name, which I have not commanded him to speak, or that shall speak in the name of other gods, even that prophet shall die" (Deuteronomy 18:20).

The Prophet Isaiah

prediction that, in future times, all the heirlooms and treasures in the temple and palace of Jerusalem will be carried off to Babylon, along with many of the king's descendants.

After the focus on immediate repentance in the first 39 chapters, the remainder of Isaiah is devoted to the future, to comforting God's people and to reassuring them of their liberation at the hands of Cyrus the Great. It tells of their gradual return to Jerusalem and of Jerusalem's future as the world's holy city. In Isaiah's writing about a "suffering servant," particularly in

Isaiah 53:5–6, Christians find a portent of Christ the Messiah: "But he *was* wounded for our transgressions, *he was* bruised for our iniquities: the chastisement of our peace was upon him; and with his stripes we are healed. All we like sheep have gone astray; we have turned every one to his own way; and the Lord hath laid on him the iniquity of us all."

Considered the "Prince of Prophets" both for his royal social standing and for the intricate mastery of his language, Isaiah's is among the most widely read books in the Bible.

THE BOOK OF
JEREMIAH

GOD MUST LITERALLY PUT WORDS INTO THE MOUTH OF THE RELUCTANT
JEREMIAH BEFORE THIS PROPHET IS ABLE TO SPREAD THE WARNINGS
OF HIS PROPHECIES TO HIS SKEPTICAL FRIENDS AND NEIGHBORS.

The Book of Jeremiah spans the reign of the five last kings of Judah and the kingdom's collapse, beginning in the thirteenth year of the reign of Josiah and ending when the Babylonians capture King Zedekiah. Throughout the twenty-fourth book of the Bible, Jeremiah's own people mock, torment, and imprison him, treating him as a traitor for speaking his prophetic words. Not only does the prophet warn his fellow citizens of the coming devastation at the hands of the Babylonians, he lives through

Jeremiah on the ruins of Jerusalem

> Before I formed thee in the belly I knew thee; and before thou camest forth out of the womb I sanctified thee, *and* I ordained thee a prophet unto the nations.
>
> JEREMIAH 1:5

the carnage of these times as well. We last hear from him 27 years after these catastrophic events, when he sends a message of hope and a future return to those now living in exile.

This book recounts how Jeremiah, the son of a Levite priest, lives on the

God commanded Jeremiah to be His prophet

people have no interest in reforming, however, and when Jeremiah realizes that there is no hope for his people, he begs the officials to surrender to the Babylonians and live peacefully under their rule—for which his community brands him a traitor and throws him into prison. As his worst prophecies come to pass, Jeremiah warns those fleeing Judah for Egypt of the utter impossibility of escaping God's wrath.

Years later, when he predicts the eventual destruction of Babylon and the return of the exiles to Jerusalem, Jeremiah brings a measure of comfort to all those living in Babylonian captivity.

outskirts of Jerusalem in the small community of Anathoth. Unlike Isaiah, Jeremiah does not want to accept God's command when He calls him to be His prophet. But God compels him to speak involuntarily, and, suddenly, Jeremiah cannot resist imploring his neighbors to correct their egregious moral and spiritual lapses before disaster strikes. When he preaches in the temple, however, he faces scorn from those who refuse to believe the great monument could ever fall.

Discouraged and lamenting his birth, Jeremiah begs God to relieve him of his duties. In protest, he resorts to symbolic actions to gain the attention of the authorities—he clamps an oxen yoke around his neck and shatters a clay jug in front of religious leaders, refusing to take part in any customs of marriage, mourning, or celebration. The

Jeremiah is called the "weeping prophet"

THE BOOK OF
LAMENTATIONS

THE AUTHOR OF LAMENTATIONS IS ANONYMOUS, BUT SCHOLARS OFTEN ATTRIBUTE IT TO THE PROPHET JEREMIAH. WITH THE AUTHOR UNKNOWN, THE BOOK ALLOWS THE READER TO IDENTIFY WITH THE GRIEF OF THE NARRATOR.

E very year, on the anniversary of the destruction of Jerusalem, those of Jewish faith read from this section of the Bible. Following the tradition of the Septuagint and Vulgate versions, these five tragic poems, mourning the catastrophic leveling of Solomon's Temple and the great city in which it stood in 586 BCE, appear directly after the Book of Jeremiah. Historians traditionally attribute Lamentations to the prophet Jeremiah, whose people meet his

The Destruction of the Temple of Jerusalem

Wherefore dost thou forget us forever, and forsake us so long a time?

LAMENTATIONS (5:20)

---

warnings of impending disaster with anger and ridicule—though the identity of the true author is unclear.

The first poem of Lamentations describes the sorrows of Jerusalem and provides an overview of the destroyed city soon after the Babylonian army levels its walls, demolishes the great temple, and carries off all its valuables and important citizens. Those who remain, left with no human allies and deserted by God, experience starvation. The narrator bitterly regrets the disobedient behavior that sparked this dire situation, considering the invading army a tool of God's rage.

Jeremiah Lamenting the Destruction of Jerusalem

The second poem recounts the dreadful consequences of invoking God's wrath. In his great anger, God levels every village of the Kingdom of Judah, and the dead litter the streets. Passages describe in great detail the invading army inflicting terror on the helpless citizens. The narrator cries out, begging God for mercy.

The narrator relates his own personal torment in the third poem, insisting that God is indeed merciful and will one day end all suffering. He reminds God of the many times in the past that He has answered prayers, and implores Him to punish his enemies.

The fourth poem considers Jerusalem after the fall, relating the disbelief of those in the surrounding territories that such destruction could ever occur. It ends with a warning to Jerusalem's neighbors, Edom and Uz, of their own impending disasters.

The Book of Lamentations closes with a prayer for mercy in the fifth and final poem—a declaration of renewed faith from a people who are begging God to return to them.

ΕΖΕ
ΚΙΑC

ΕΖΕ
ΚΙΑC

THE BOOK OF
EZEKIEL

WHILE CAPTIVE IN BABYLON, EZEKIEL HAS GREAT VISIONS
AND COMMUNICATES WITH GOD. A FOREFATHER OF JUDAISM,
EZEKIEL IS ONE OF THE BIBLE'S MOST IMPORTANT PROPHETS.

Ezekiel's name, which means "God strengthens," is prophetic itself, for Ezekiel was uncompromising in delivering God's judgments. This prophet did a great deal to fortify the laws of Jewish worship, influencing the way it is practiced today, and many scholars call him "the father of the Jewish religion."

Babylon had taken prominent citizens and royalty of Judah captive several times before Nebuchadnezzar finally leveled it in 586 BCE. Ezekiel was among the three thousand nobles forced into exile in 597 BCE, along with King Jehoiachin. As a priest, he ministered to the Jewish community along the Chebar River in Babylon. At the age of thirty, six years before the great destruction of the temple, he received his first vision and calling as a prophet.

The Book of Ezekiel is written in the first person; God refers to Ezekiel as "Mortal Man." Unlike earlier prophets, who feel physically compelled to speak the words of God they receive, Ezekiel has elaborate visions filled with

incredible imagery. God first appears to Ezekiel driving through the sky on a blindingly bright chariot adorned with cherubs. He tells Ezekiel to eat a scroll with God's words on it. At one point he animates and brings to life a field of dead human bones. God gives him the responsibility of being "the Watchman." Ezekiel utilizes symbolic actions, such as drawings on clay tiles or cutting and burning his hair, to best communicate with his community and warn them.

Ezekiel firmly believed that it is the duty of all nations—not just Israel—to obey God and observe His rules, and a portion of the Book of Ezekiel alerts neighboring countries to their impending punishment for apostasy. Following the great destruction of the nation and the prediction of resettlement, God declares that, going forward, the Kingdoms of Judah and Israel will once again be one nation. The book relates a vision of how the new temple is to be built, as well as the religious laws that the people must follow. Ezekiel ends with a survey of the resettled nation and the manner in which the Twelve Tribes will divide the land among themselves.

OPPOSITE PAGE: *Ezekiel's Prayer*

Visions of Ezekiel

AN INSPIRATION FOR THOUSANDS OF YEARS TO ARTISTS, POETS, AND WRITERS, EZEKIEL'S ASTONISHING VISIONS, WITH THEIR FANTASTICAL IMAGERY, NEARLY DEFY DESCRIPTION.

When God first appears to Ezekiel and calls him to service, the Bible's narrator struggles to convey the grandeur of the apparition that he observes. He describes a glowing sky with lightning and a windstorm. At its center are four winged creatures in human form, each with four different faces—a man, a bull, a lion, and an

> And when the living creatures went,
> the wheels went by them;
> and when the living creatures were lifted up
> from the earth, the wheels were lifted up.
>
> EZEKIEL 1:19

eagle. These creatures control the wheels of a flaming chariot, surrounded by cherubs, which

lands on Earth carrying a sapphire throne atop a crystal dome. Sitting on the throne

Mystic Wheel, as envisioned by Ezekiel

is a bronze-like human being emanating light rays of every color of the rainbow. This first vision of God heavily influences Revelation; the parts of the four-winged creatures became the artistic symbols for each of the Four Evangelists: Matthew, Mark, Luke, and John.

Ezekiel's second vision transports him to the Temple of Jerusalem. God shows Ezekiel the idols that have occupied it and has him break a hole in the wall, where he witnesses the secret worship of pagan gods in a room filled with images. Ezekiel then sees other men, their backs to the sanctuary, bowing to the rising sun. God, outraged, abandons the temple, enabling its future destruction.

The story of God and Ezekiel in the Valley of Dry Bones

is, perhaps, one of the most fantastic in the entire Bible. God orders Ezekiel to "prophesy upon" the bones, which are spread on the ground as far as the eye can see. As Ezekiel tells the bones that God is going to prove he is the sovereign lord by giving them new life, they begin to rattle, forming into skeletons; muscle and skin begin to cover them. When the wind blows, Ezekiel finds standing before him an army of living, breathing men, and God tells him that the people of Israel are like these men—ready to be resuscitated to begin a new life.

In Ezekiel's final vision, God again takes him to the site of the temple in Jerusalem, providing details for its reconstruction.

The Vision of the Valley of the Dry Bones

Ezekiel's vision of the rebuilding of Jerusalem

OPPOSITE PAGE: *The Vision of Ezekiel*

THE BOOK OF
DANIEL

LIKE EZEKIEL, THE BOOK OF DANIEL TAKES PLACE ENTIRELY IN BABYLON.
EVEN SO, DANIEL RETAINS HIS JEWISH IDENTITY AND DIETARY CUSTOMS,
ULTIMATELY IMPRESSING HIS CAPTORS WITH HIS DEVOTION TO GOD.

While prophetic writings are general in nature, and hinge on the moral behavior of society, apocalyptic warnings are inevitable, unchanging, and precise. In an interesting twist, the Christian Bible considers Daniel prophetic, whereas the Hebrew Bible recognizes his predictions as apocalyptic writing.

The first section of Daniel is a third-person account portraying the abduction of Judah's noble families by Babylon's King Nebuchadnezzar. The royal court judges Daniel and his three young friends to be superior and selects them to serve their captors. Excellent students and respectful of the king, they nevertheless secretly retain their

Hanging Gardens of the Semiramis

Jewish identity. When Nebuchadnezzar has a troubling dream, and none of the court wizards can interpret it, he orders everyone at court executed. Daniel prays to God and receives the answer, earning promotion, wealth, and royal admiration. When Daniel's friends refuse to worship a gold statue in the desert, however, the Babylonians throw them into a furnace. They are spared when an angel saves them.

Daniel retains his high position, even after Darius the Mede overthrows the kingdom, but when Darius catches Daniel praying to God, he reluctantly enforces a law punishing such worship. Darius throws Daniel into a lion's den, but, when he finds Daniel unharmed the next day, he is overjoyed, proclaiming great respect for Daniel's God.

Israel's guardian, and—in what many Christians consider a prediction of the end of the world—the resurrection of the dead for final judgment concludes the book.

Scholars believe that the Book of Daniel was, in fact, written around 165 BCE, during the persecution of Antiochus Epiphanes, many years after

Daniel's Answer to the King

> I make a decree, That in every dominion of my kingdom men tremble and fear before the God of Daniel: for he *is* the living God, and steadfast for ever, and his kingdom *that* which shall not be destroyed, and his dominion *shall be even* unto the end.
>
> DANIEL 6:26

The second part of the book of Daniel consists of first-person accounts of his visions. With the help of the Archangel Gabriel, who acts as interpreter, Daniel predicts the rise and fall of four great empires, as well as the incredible oppression of God's people and their ultimate deliverance. Archangel Michael takes his place as

the Babylonian captivity. By recalling a dreadful time in their earlier history, the author of Daniel encourages his persecuted people to stay strong; the fact that many of the earlier prophecies had proven true in hindsight makes plausible, for contemporary readers, the book's prediction regarding the ultimate triumph of good over evil.

THE BOOK OF
HOSEA

THE BOOK OF HOSEA OFFERS A DIFFERENT SIDE OF GOD,
DEPICTING HIM AS A LOVING, PARENTAL FIGURE, RELUCTANTLY
HANDING OUT PUNISHMENT TO HIS DISTANT, COMBATIVE CHILDREN.

The prophet Hosea preached to the Northern Kingdom of Israel during the years of that nation's great decline, just before Assyria conquered it in 721 BCE. Like the prophets to the south, Hosea warned his fellow citizens against forgetting their culture and religion at a time when the northern tribes had completely given themselves over to the worship of their neighbors' gods of fertility. Though their priests paid lip service to the religious rites, they did not strictly uphold the laws in Deuteronomy or show proper respect to God and His covenant. A contemporary of Isaiah in the south, Hosea issued warnings that are similarly stern about God's coming punishment. Yet, the Book of Hosea depicts God in a new light: as a loving, frustrated parent who can scarcely bear to mete out the justice his belligerent children deserve.

> And I will sow her unto me in the earth; and I will have mercy upon her that had not obtained mercy; and I will say *to them which were* not my people, Thou *art* my people; and they shall say, *Thou art* my God.
>
> HOSEA 2:23

Mountain landscape with river valley and the prophet Hosea

The first part of Hosea is a parable devoted to the prophet's marriage to an unfaithful wife, Gomer, who represents the treacherous nation of Israel in its relationship to God. Hosea and Gomer have a son, who God names Jezreel after

Hosea shows God to be merciful

them will live apart for a while, until a time when they can be reunited. The book ends on a similarly positive note as God declares His love for his people and promises a future reconciliation.

For Hosea, God is stern but loving

the valley in which Jehu assassinated the King of Israel one hundred years earlier, taking power and founding a new dynasty. Their second child is a daughter—God names her Unloved, because He is about to disown His people. Their third child, another son, goes by Not My People—as God says of Israel, "They are not my people and I am not their God."

The people fail to heed Hosea's warnings, and melancholy tinges his musings about God. Unlike previous prophets, who predicted fire and brimstone as revenge and a rebuke to those who stray, Hosea views God as a loving and merciful force who will enforce His punishment as a form of correction, if only to bring His people back into His fold. Because God values justice, He must reprimand wrongdoing. When Hosea's wife leaves him to become a prostitute, God commands Hosea to buy her back. Hosea informs Gomer that the two of

THE BOOK OF
JOEL

JOEL, LIKE THE OTHER PROPHETS, COMPELS HIS PEOPLE TO FIND HUMILITY AND HONOR THEIR DEBT TO GOD. GOD ONCE AGAIN PROVES HIS DEVOTION TO THE CHOSEN PEOPLE, GRANTING MERCY IN EXCHANGE FOR OBEDIENCE.

Historians know little about the prophet Joel, for whom the twenty-ninth book of the Bible is named. Addressed to the people of the Southern Kingdom of Judah, the Book of Joel appears to date from the time of Uzziah, one of the great kings, who reigned from 792 to 740 BCE. It was a time of great prosperity: Judah's neighbors respected its borders, its crops were successful, and the people indulged themselves extravagantly.

Written as a poem, the opening of Joel places us immediately in the midst of a swarm of locusts. Judah is suffering the invasion of this insect army, which has come out of nowhere to decimate grapevines, crops, and fruit trees. Everything the people have been taking for granted is instantly destroyed.

Joel announces that this nuisance is a message from God—unless the people repent and reassess their lives, they will witness even greater destruction.

The people, terrified, realize that there is nothing left to sacrifice to God. Joel orders them to go to the temple and repent with all their hearts. He repeatedly warns them about God's ultimate judgment, saying, "The day of the Lord is coming."

God reacts to the people's pleas with mercy, restoring fertility to the land. God then speaks of a time when His spirit will pour out on everyone, regardless of age or sex. The New Testament refers to this outpouring of spiritual enlightenment many times; it is a form of blessing available to all people, Jews and Gentiles alike. Joel

> And it shall come to pass afterward, that I will pour out my spirit upon all flesh; and your sons and your daughters shall prophesy, your old men shall dream dreams, your young men shall see visions.
>
> JOEL 2:28

The Prophet Joel

becomes known as the "Prophet of the Pentecost," an allusion to the fact that God first pours out His spirit at the time of Shavuot, a date Christians later honor analogously as the Pentecost.

The Book of Joel ends with God describing the Valley of Judgment, where thousands of citizens of neighboring nations will go to be punished for their maltreatment of His people. As God promises to obtain justice for Judah and Jerusalem, he also vows to remain forever on Mount Zion, ruling over an idyllic world.

THE BOOK OF
AMOS

DATING BACK TO THE EIGHTH CENTURY BCE, AMOS IS THE EARLIEST PROPHETIC
RECORD IN THE BIBLE. AMOS, TOO, SEES BLEAK CONSEQUENCES FOR HIS
PEOPLE—BUT AN AMENDMENT PREDICTS ISRAEL WILL RISE AGAIN.

Amos rebukes Israel's luxury

Amos was a working farmer and herder. His warnings and judgments contain many details of the daily life of his times, related from the viewpoint of a man thoroughly disgusted with his contemporaries' casual acceptance of injustice.

The Book of Amos begins as God gives Amos his mandate, telling him of the disastrous future awaiting each of Israel's neighbor countries. Though Amos is from Judah, God orders him to go to the Northern Kingdom of Israel to issue his warnings. Amos, who believes God belongs to everyone and is not Israel's deity alone, groups Judah, accordingly, with the nations that have earned God's wrath.

The book explains in great detail why God is so enraged with Israel: not only has the nation blatantly neglected its religious practice, but the rich are also immorally exploiting the poor. Because the rich can afford to give sacrifices in the temples, they assume God will keep His covenant with them by continuing to reward them materially while

The Prophet Amos gave up being a farmer to become a prophet

punishing the poor, who, of course, cannot make similar sacrifices.

When Amos tells the high priest in the Northern Kingdom that ritualistic observances are worthless to God in the face of such institutionalized injustice, the king's aides report him as a troublemaker and subsequently order him to return to Judah. Amos states that he is in the kingdom on God's mission—he simply cannot and will not accept dismissal.

Amos foresees the total destruction of Israel, during which plagues of locusts will destroy the fields and fire ravage the land. He sees a plumb line dangling, out of balance. God's people, who, like the plumb line, are equally out of balance, must make themselves upright. In Amos's final vision, he sees a basket of ripe fruit, which he interprets as a symbol of the country's prosperity at its height; in the next phase, he foretells there will be decay and rot.

God's own words fill the last chapter of Amos: He promises to punish Israel, leveling her cities and killing most of the populace, preserving only the select few who follow His word. Scholars suggest that the book's authors much later added a final paragraph, predicting the future restoration of Israel.

WAR AND WARFARE

The biblical era, from Old to New Testament times, was filled with violence and war, but the Bible goes into little specific detail about particular wars or battles beyond the reason for fighting and the results of the skirmishes.

BEFORE KING DAVID'S REIGN, Israel relied on tribal militia—local men, called into service when needed, who were willing to fight to the death to protect their homes and families, but also just as willing to leave a battle to return to their land for the harvest. King David, intent on building an empire, greatly advanced Israel's military strategy by recruiting full-time mercenary soldiers and copying the battle tactics of his most powerful enemies. He took charge of manufacturing metal weapons and shields to better outfit his army. Geographically, biblical Israel was destined to frequently become a battlefield, for it straddled major trade routes between Sumeria, Assyria, and Egypt.

The Sumerians developed the battle chariots used in Mesopotamia in the first half of the third millennium BCE.

Israelites carried captive

Egypt followed suit some twelve hundred years later. Carrying an armed soldier and a driver and pulled through open battle zones at top speed by pairs of horses, the chariots terrified foot soldiers. King Solomon kept a large chariot squadron at his disposal, and they swelled in popularity under Ahab, King of Israel, whose chariot force numbered two thousand at the Battle of Ramoth-Gilead.

The War against Gibeon

Siege warfare, though expensive and time-consuming, was the most effective method when attackers were few in number. The Assyrians built zigzag trenches to safely reach the walls of a besieged city; engineers invented battering rams and mining tools to open walls. The attackers would encircle the city with their army, keeping watch for attempted escapes, while the engineers constructed siege ramps of earth and wood to better position their battering rams. The inhabitants of the city, trapped inside during this long process, often starved to death while waiting for the breach of the wall, which would bring either horrible slaughter or enslavement. The Babylonians constructed 45 wooden towers to allow their army to scale the walls of Jerusalem.

The Bible spells out specific rules of engagement: for example, one must ask God if it is wise to do battle. Armies must request that the enemy surrender peacefully—if the enemy does surrender, then God's people must do no harm. Soldiers must keep encampments, considered a place of God, clean. Victors must execute kings and rulers of conquered peoples, and destroy all pagan artifacts.

Sumerian war chariot

THE BOOK OF
OBADIAH

THE BOOK OF OBADIAH IS A WARNING TO THE NEIGHBORING NATIONS OF JUDAH THAT DO NOT FOLLOW THE SECOND COMMANDMENT. FOR EDOM, IN PARTICULAR, GOD WARNS OF AN ALLY DESTROYING THE NATION.

The name Obadiah means "servant of God," and it is in God's voice that the prophet writes, in just 21 verses, a bitter, angry denunciation of Edom and its people. A neighboring nation of Judah, the inhabitants of Edom were direct descendants of Esau via his twin brother Jacob, and related by blood to the Judeans. The Book of Obadiah primarily addresses the subject of

God appearing to Obadiah in his dream

Edom's punishment for its uncharitable conduct toward Judah.

We know little about Obadiah, but scholars speculate that his book dates from the time of the fall of Jerusalem in 586 BCE. Instead of coming to their neighbor's aid, the unsympathetic Edomites gloat and mock their distant cousins, even as they loot the city, reveling in its destruction and downfall. The behavior of the Edomites enrages God, even though He does not consider them His people, for they have not followed the second commandment, "to love thy neighbor as thyself." God warns Edom not to be so confident about its defenses—He will see that a trusted friend and trading partner turns on them and destroys their nation.

The next section of Obadiah addresses the other nations surrounding Judah. All are doomed to vanish; eventually, the returning exiles will resettle their lands. Those from Judah will occupy Edom and Philistia; returning Israelites from the north will take over Phoenicia and Zarephath, as well as Ephraim and Samaria. Though many passages in the Bible consist of

DESTRUCCIO IHEROSOLIME

Destruction of Jerusalem

the prophets warning Israel about its coming chastisement, it is God who will deliver their punishment, Obadiah who, remaining in Jerusalem, have been repeatedly victimized and humiliated. There will be a judgment

---

For the day of the Lord is near upon all the heathen:
as thou hast done, it shall be done unto thee:
thy reward shall return upon thine own head.

OBADIAH 1:15

---

says. No nation may take advantage of another's suffering.

Even as Obadiah stands as a warning to hostile neighboring countries, the book also serves to reassure those day, they are given to understand—and, equally important, God's people must acknowledge that they alone will not be triumphant, for God Himself will be king of all nations.

THE BOOK OF
JONAH

JONAH, RELUCTANT TO ACCEPT HIS ROLE AS PROPHET, TRIES TO ESCAPE HIS FATE, BUT GOD CHASES HIM OUT TO SEA. SWALLOWED BY A WHALE, JONAH ACCEPTS HIS GIFT AND BEGINS TO PREACH SALVATION.

RIGHT: Jonah and the Whale

Told in the third person, the Book of Jonah differs from the other prophetic books of the Bible. The name Jonah means "dove," and as a prophet, Jonah proves as passive as his namesake—so reluctant to take on God's mandate to preach salvation that he runs away in an attempt to avoid Him. Yet, much to his own disappointment, Jonah goes on to become one of the most successful prophets in the Bible.

As Jonah opens, God orders the prophet to travel to Ninevah, the great capital of Assyria, to speak out against the lawless and licentious behavior of

Jonah leaves the Whale's belly

its citizens. Instead of doing what God orders, however, Jonah runs away, boarding a ship. God pursues Jonah while he is at sea, sending a strong wind that threatens to break up the boat. As the sailors pray to their gods, Jonah goes below to sleep in the ship's hold. When the sailors draw lots to determine who is causing this problem, Jonah's name comes up. The sailors bring him up on deck, and Jonah confesses that

*Jonah preaches
to the Ninevites*

he is running from God; he advises the sailors to throw him overboard to stop the storm. They do so reluctantly, and the seas immediately calm. A large whale then swallows Jonah, and he stays in its belly for three days. In the second chapter of the book, Jonah says a prayer from deep inside the whale, ending with the words, "Salvation comes from the Lord!" As he utters these words, the whale spits him out onto the shore.

Chastened, Jonah travels to Ninevah, where he tells the people God will destroy them in forty days unless they repent. The people, believing Jonah's message, repent and beg for forgiveness. God elects not to punish them, thereby angering Jonah, who feels God has made a fool of him, making him travel so far only to have his prophecy go unfulfilled. When Jonah rests in the sun, God creates a giant shade plant to shield him. The next day God sends a worm to destroy the plant, and when Jonah expresses his sorrow and protests the loss of the plant, God says He would be far more sorry to have killed all the 120,000 residents of Ninevah.

THE BOOK OF
MICAH

MICAH CHAMPIONS THE POOR AND SICK AND CRITICIZES
THOSE LEADERS AND CITIZENS WHO TURN A BLIND EYE TO
THE SUFFERING OF THOSE LESS FORTUNATE.

A contemporary of Isaiah, the prophet Micah lived in a small town in Judah in the Southern Kingdom. While Isaiah preached from a position of power in the city, Micah preached from a rural base among the poor and humble; his immediate concern was for the safety of the little villages on the outskirts of Judah.

Of all the prophets, Micah expressed the most outrage at the treatment of the poverty-stricken and weak by the wealthy landowners of their own tribe.

Micah prophesies Judgment and Nativity

He blamed these unfair social and economic conditions for the coming judgment of God. Assyria had overrun the Northern Kingdom by this time, and Micah was convinced that Judah and Jerusalem would suffer the same fate. Unlike Isaiah, who held to the belief that the temple would always stand, Micah foresaw a day when both the temple and all of Judah would fall.

The first three of seven chapters in Micah are devoted to God's judgment on Israel and Jerusalem. God promises to reduce to rubble the capital of Samaria in Israel; Micah says he will mourn it and warns Jerusalem of its own impending doom. In scathing language, Micah denounces Israel's leaders for listening to false prophets—they are as corrupt as the officials in the government who exploit the poor and insist that God is with them.

In the fourth chapter, Micah, like Isaiah, foresees a future where peace reigns on earth. The people will rebuild Jerusalem as a place where God truly dwells and "nations will never go again to war." God will protect the new nation when Israel returns from exile.

The Prophet Micah

Christians see the often-cited fifth chapter of Micah as a prediction of Jesus as the Messiah: in it, God promises to send from Bethlehem a ruler whose

In the sixth chapter, the prophet insists that the best way to worship God is not through ritual but by living with love, justice, and respect for one

And he shall stand and feed in the strength of the Lord,
in the majesty of the name of the Lord his God;
and they shall abide: for now shall he be great unto
the ends of the earth.

MICAH 5:4

bloodlines go back to ancient times. People from all over the world will follow this ruler, once He takes the throne, for He will bring peace.

another. Micah ends on a positive note, with promises of redemption and a prayer praising God for keeping faith with His people going back to Abraham.

THE BOOK OF
NAHUM AND HABAKKUK

BOTH THE BOOK OF NAHUM AND THE BOOK OF HABAKKUK CENTER ON THE BABYLONIAN TAKEOVER OF ASSYRIA. NAHUM CELEBRATES THE FALL OF NINEVAH, WHILE HABAKKUK DETAILS THE CRUEL TREATMENT OF THE JUDEANS.

RIGHT: The Prophet Nahum

Nahum and Habakkuk make an interesting juxtaposition. Nahum is essentially a poem celebrating the destruction of the city of Ninevah by the Babylonians, while Habakkuk is a conversation between

> The Lord *is* slow to anger, and great in power, and will not at all acquit *the wicked*: the Lord hath his way in the whirlwind and in the storm, and the clouds *are* the dust of his feet.
>
> NAHUM 1:3

God and the prophet Habakkuk about the horrible treatment the Judeans suffer at the hands of the Babylonians. Nahum considers the Babylonians a tool of God's wrath against Assyria,

while Habakkuk continually asks God why these cruel people always seem to triumph.

The name Nahum comes from the Hebrew word for "comforter," and it is probable that the book of Nahum dates from the time of the fall of Ninevah, in 612 BCE, not before—in which case, it is not a true prophecy.

Assyria is an overwhelmingly powerful nation, and Ninevah, its capital, seems impenetrable, but Nahum, in his vision, lists all the ways in which invading forces bring low and destroy the city and its residents.

During Habakkuk's life, he says, he witnessed a good king, Josiah, killed in battle with the Egyptians, who then went on to capture the rightful heir to the throne and install a weak and corrupt ruler in his place.

> Why dost thou shew me iniquity, and cause me to behold grievance? for spoiling and violence are before me: and there are that raise up strife and contention.
>
> HABAKKUK 1:3

Nahum calls on all the residents of Judah to celebrate this divine act of justice, giving them hope that God is truly protecting them.

Writing just a few years later, Habakkuk, also from Judah, is horrified at the military success of the Babylonians, who seem to be triumphing over the righteous with impunity. When he questions why this should be so, God tells Habakkuk that in order to teach all the nations a lesson, He plans to make the Babylonian army the greatest force in the world. The next time Habakkuk begs for an answer, God assures him that—eventually—evil will not triumph; if people live righteously and well, they will flourish because they have remained faithful to God.

Yet, Habakkuk boldly demands to know why God allows such terrible injustices to happen to righteous people. Why are those who behave so abominably, as the Babylonians do, allowed to dominate time and again?

The situation in Judah is quickly deteriorating at the time Habakkuk writes this dialogue, but despite the chaos swirling around him, and whatever his misgivings, Habakkuk ends with a prayer asking God for strength.

The Prophet Habakkuk

THE BOOK OF
ZEPHANIAH

THE BOOK OF ZEPHANIAH IS THE LAST PROPHETIC BOOK BEFORE
THE BABYLONIAN INVASION AND THE EXILE OF THE JEWS FROM ISRAEL.

RIGHT: Icon of Zephaniah

The name Zephaniah means "defended by God," and the Book of Zephaniah likely dates back to the reign of King Josiah, written a decade before he enacts the religious reforms of 622 BCE. According to the opening lines, Zephaniah, a contemporary of the prophet Jeremiah, is a descendant of Hezekiah, possibly the greatest King of Judah. For this reason, some believe that Zephaniah's unpopular message was very likely heard in the royal circles of his day.

Although Zephaniah reiterates some of the other prophets' complaints—the people have strayed far from the original covenant, and God will severely punish them for their wicked behavior—Zephaniah also states his belief that Israel must set a moral example for the world, acting as if Israel is God's representative on earth. Viewing the coming catastrophe not as a local but as a world event, Zephaniah says that God will hold all nations accountable for their behavior, including those He has used in the past to punish His people. God reminds Zephaniah that He has visited destruction on Earth's inhabitants

before—only to watch His people grow into a population of morally weak and corrupt money and idol worshippers, ignorant of the laws He has handed down. He predicts that He will be compelled to repeat this apocalyptic act, sparing no country. The few people left in each land will pray

Josiah, King of Judah

only to Him—He alone will be every nation's God. Zephaniah ends with a joyful psalm celebrating a future where

Jerusalem is the center of the world, with exiles returning to a land of peace showered in God's love.

Ironically, it is during the reign of King Josiah that a copy of the laws of Deuteronomy appears in the temple.

Josiah, realizing how far the Israelites had wandered from their initial covenant with God, attempts to correct their course by enacting major religious reforms. These are short-lived, however; after his death the nation again lapses into its previous state of profound religious indifference.

(L–R) Zephaniah, Joel, Obadiah, Hosea

ANIMALS IN THE BIBLE

From beasts of burden, crucial to performing work and transporting goods across the unforgiving biblical landscape—to creatures with more symbolic significance, such as dogs and whales—the Bible contains references to a host of animals.

IN GENESIS, GOD CREATES man last, after the birds, fishes, and land animals over which humankind receives dominion. The Middle East had many lush forests at the time the Bible was written; it was home to countless animal species, some now extremely rare—as the forests are also. Humanity depended on animals for food, clothing, and transportation.

Of the Bible's beasts of burden—including horses (used primarily in warfare), camels,

Abraham's Journey from Ur to Canaan

Destruction of the Leviathan

and oxen—the donkey, or ass, is the most prized; the Bible mentions it more than 130 times. Its intelligence, strength, surefootedness, and agility were perfectly suited for the Holy Land's rough, hilly terrain. Ridden by people of every social status, it carried heavy loads of household goods and trade items. The donkeys of Damascus were the ideal breed—caravans of five or six hundred and as many as three thousand were constantly entering and leaving the city the Assyrians referred to as the "city of the asses." Abraham led his tribe to the Promised Land with

Adoration of the Lamb

symbol of war. It is on an ass that Jesus rides into Jerusalem.

The people raised sheep, goats, and cattle for meat and milk; their wool, hair, and skins generated everything from clothing to liquid containers. Because the Bible lists them as "clean," teachings permitted these three animals for sacrifice. A fatted calf or goat was essential to religious feasts. In the New Testament, the Gospel of John proclaims that Jesus is the "Lamb of God."

Of the "unclean" animals the Bible forbids as food, according to Hebrew law in Leviticus 11 and Deuteronomy 14, the swine (pig) is filthiest; the most degrading job

Lion, symbol of the tribe of Judah

such a caravan, and the Hebrews considered the ass the emblem of peace, just as the horse was the

is swineherd. For its behavior, people then considered the dog vile. Shepherds used trained dogs to keep wild animals away from the flock, but the biblical specimen is clearly not "man's best friend."

Though now extinct in the region, lions were, in biblical times, prevalent in the Holy Land. Solomon greatly admired them for their strength, power, and dignity, and even decorated his temple with their likeness. Lions were also the symbol of the tribe of Judah.

Snakes, also common, were of course considered symbols of evil dating from their first appearance in the Garden of Eden. The Bible also frequently cites the Leviathan, a monster of the sea— most likely a whale.

Jesus riding into Jerusalem

THE BOOKS OF
HAGGAI AND ZECHARIAH

BOTH THE BOOK OF HAGGAI AND THE BOOK OF ZECHARIAH REVOLVE AROUND THE PROPHETS' DIRECTIVE TO INSPIRE THE EXILES TO REBUILD GOD'S TEMPLE IN JERUSALEM.

God gave Haggai and Zechariah the task of rallying the returned exiles in Jerusalem—the common people as well as officialdom—and energizing both groups to complete work on the second temple after many years' cessation. In Ezra 5:1, they are responsible for notifying the governor and the high priests of Jerusalem of the universal importance of this work.

The Book of Haggai is the first prophetic book written following the Jews' return from captivity. The authors completed the prophecies within four months, spanning August to December 520 BCE.

Work begun on the reconstruction of the temple in 536 BCE had since been suspended, the result of political intrigue and infighting amongst the newly returned exiles. God commands Haggai to go directly to the governor and announce to the people that the time for procrastination has ended. He points out that although the returnees have all built fine houses for themselves, they have indeed neglected to create a home for God. Haggai also notes that the people are getting by on just enough food and

RIGHT: The Prophet Haggai

Zechariah's Vision of Four Chariots

drink—there has been no real prosperity in the years since their return.

Speaking for God, the prophet Haggai guarantees a major improvement in the community's standard of living as soon as it completes the temple. God also tells Haggai that although the second temple will not look as glorious as the first, disappointing some, it will nevertheless be filled with God's glory, and the lord of hosts will bring peace. (Because the second temple was destroyed by Rome in 70 CE, Christians believe that it is Christ who brings God's glory into the second temple.)

Though the Book of Zechariah is the longest and most complicated book of the minor prophets, it perfectly complements Haggai in its mission and placement in the Bible. In a series of visions, Zechariah concerns himself with the need for repentance and the necessity of God's people to return to His laws. God, promising to bring His people back from wherever they have scattered, says the future king of Jerusalem will be of humble birth, arriving on a donkey. New Testament writers cite for inspiration the frequent messianic predictions in Zechariah, as well as his apocalyptic visions of God's final judgment, which end the book.

THE BOOK OF
MALACHI

THE BOOK OF MALACHI IS BOTH THE LAST BOOK OF THE PROPHETS AND THE FINAL BOOK IN THE OLD TESTAMENT. MALACHI ACTS AS AN ORACLE FOR GOD—HIS NAME EVEN MEANS "GOD'S MESSENGER."

Written in the years after Nehemiah returns to Persia (approximately 433 BCE), the Book of Malachi is the last book of Prophets. Jerusalem has been resettled for almost one hundred years; Nehemiah has rebuilt the city walls. Yet Jerusalem remains an outpost of the Persian Empire, not the glorious crossroads of the world the other prophets envisioned. The temple, though rebuilt, does not seem imbued with God's spirit, nor is it the envy of the surrounding nations, as Solomon's once was.

The tepid tone of religious worship reflects the people's general malaise.

The coming of God's messenger

They mistrust the covenant with God and do not take His laws seriously. Those who break them for material and social gain do not seem to suffer repercussions for their actions.

The Book of Malachi narrates an imagined conversation between God and his people. When the people doubt God's love because they are experiencing hard times, he reminds them of worse situations in other countries—notably Edom, where he obviously does not favor its inhabitants, the descendants of Esau. The priests realize that, instead of the best specimens in a flock, they are sacrificing inferior animals to God. Men are leaving the wives of their youth and remarrying, thereby breaking their vows—not only to their first wives, but also to God. God uses these examples to decry the unfaithfulness of all the people, reminding them that they are subject to His final judgment. He requires the people to stop cheating and pay tithes to the temple, demanding what is rightfully His. When the people ask God why evil prospers without punishment and the just always seem to struggle, God calls upon His doubters to cease, assuring them that there is a book in which He records the names of the just; on the day of the Lord, the evil will burn like straw.

At the conclusion of Malachi, God informs His people that before the day of the Lord arrives, He will send the prophet Elijah back to earth, and they will be rewarded for following the laws and commandments He gave to Moses.

The Prophet Malachi

The Apocrypha

Found neither in the Hebrew or Protestant versions of the Bible, the Apocrypha is part of the Roman Catholic canon. Based on Jerome's translation of 382 CE, the work includes 14 books from the Greek version of the Old Testament that are not in the Hebrew version. Historians have long disputed the origin of the material that makes up the Apocrypha. As a result, the adjective *apocryphal*, meaning "of doubtful authenticity," has, over time, become part of the language. And indeed, Jews and Protestants consider these books to be based on legend rather than on the revealed word of God.

Some of the books add to previous entries (Daniel, Jeremiah, and Esther), while others, such as 1 and 2 Maccabees, are complete histories. There are dramatic stories, such as Tobit and Judith, and books of wisdom literature, such as Ecclesiasticus. The Apocrypha also includes a book of ethical teachings by Sirach, and Wisdom, which scholars attribute to Solomon. The writings of Maccabees and Ecclesiasticus date from the second century BCE, a period when there are no Hebrew Old Testament writings. Apocrypha serves as an interesting bridge between the Old and New Testaments, however dubious its provenance.

Tobit accusing Anna of stealing the kid

Judith and Susanna

JUDITH AND SUSANNA ARE BOTH BRAVE WOMEN WHO BRUSH AGAINST POWERFUL, LESS RIGHTEOUS MEN, YET THEY STILL PREVAIL.

The Book of Judith takes place during a time of Assyrian aggression. General Holofernes, having successfully destroyed the surrounding nations, is now laying siege to Judea. The town of Bethalia is about to surrender when Judith, a beautiful, wise, and wealthy widow, hatches a plan to save the country. Dressed in her finest clothes and wearing her best jewelry, she presents herself to General Holofernes, offering information in exchange for her life. Holofernes, delighted to meet such a beautiful woman, invites her into his tent. When he is drunk on wine, Judith decapitates him, bringing home his head in triumph, and the Assyrians flee.

Susanna and the Elders

Judith beheads General Holofernes

The story of Susanna and the Elders is sometimes placed as chapter 13 in the Book of Daniel. Two older judges spy Susanna, a beautiful young wife, bathing in her yard. Propositioning her, they threaten her with disgrace if she refuses them. The authorities arrest her, and a judge accuses her of committing adultery. Susanna's only hope at trial is to call on God for deliverance. Daniel provides exculpatory testimony as she is being taken out for execution, and the judge condemns the elders instead.

Bel and the Dragon/Tobit

DANIEL UNCOVERS A RUSE AND SLAYS A DRAGON,
BUT THE PEOPLE STILL PUNISH HIM. TOBIT
MIRACULOUSLY REVERSES HIS BLINDNESS.

In this supplemental fourteenth chapter to the Book of Daniel, the prophet solves a mystery: how is the idol of the god Bel eating the sacrifices laid out for him? By scattering ash on the temple floor, Daniel proves that, in reality, it is the priests and their families who are coming out of a secret room and taking the food. The king, as punishment for this ruse, orders the temple destroyed and the priests executed. Next, Daniel poisons

Tobias and the Angel

Bel and the Dragon

and kills a dragon the people are worshiping. Distraught, the people throw Daniel into the lions' den—but miraculously, six days later, they find him there completely unharmed.

The Book of Tobit begins in Ninevah. Tobit, struck blind, wants to die. His son Tobias undertakes a journey to collect money; the Archangel Raphael

joins him as a guide. Reaching his destination in Media he finds Sarah, who has, on her seven wedding nights, lost each of her husbands to a curse placed by Asmodeus, the demon of lust. With Raphael's help, Tobias catches a fish and uses its gall to break the curse. Tobias and Sarah marry and cure Tobit's blindness with the fish gall.

The Book of Wisdom

WISDOM IS A THEME THAT APPEARS CONSTANTLY IN THE OLD TESTAMENT. THE WISDOM OF KINGS AND PROPHETS IS SECOND ONLY TO GOD'S.

Attributed to Solomon, an anonymous Hellenic Jew actually wrote the Book of Wisdom late in the first century BCE. Like Solomon, the author honors the quality of wisdom, which he personifies as female, above all other traits. She is with God from eternity, sharing His throne and emanating from His thoughts. With God when He creates the world, wisdom is available to all humanity.

The first nine of the book's 19 chapters are concerned with the philosophical necessity of inviting wisdom into one's life. Rulers and kings, in particular, must seek her out. The book notes the unhappiness of those who live without wisdom, and also observes that without wisdom, there can be no justice.

The following ten chapters tell stories of the ancient ancestors, from Adam through Moses, prospering and surviving through their attainment of wisdom. The book describes the foolishness of idol worship and reminds God's people that they escaped Egypt due to the great wisdom of Aaron and Moses, while Egypt, meanwhile, suffers in darkness.

Christians recognize and praise these qualities, too, in the New Testament. Embodied by the Holy Spirit, wisdom is a force and a light emanating from God.

The Judgment of Solomon

Sirach/Baruch

THESE PORTIONS OF THE APOCRYPHA WARN, AGAIN, ABOUT THE RISKS OF PROMOTING DECADENCE WHILE IGNORING GOD.

Ecclesiasticus, also referred to as "the Wisdom of Jesus, Son of Sirach," was composed in 175 BCE and translated into Greek in 132 BCE. As in Proverbs, the author uses maxims to convey the importance of attaining wisdom, showing the path to a happy, secure life through God. Written at a time when the upper classes in Jerusalem society

Baruch writes Jeremiah's prophecies

Baruch reads to the exiled

affected Hellenic ways because they considered Greek culture superior to that of the Jews, the author attempts to remind his fellow citizens to put the God of Israel first and encourages them to be more diligent in their faith.

The secretary of the prophet Jeremiah wrote the Book of Baruch while in exile in Babylon, five years after the destruction of Jerusalem. In the first part of the book, Baruch reads to the exiled, including King Jehoiachin, describing what led to the great calamity, which he regards as

God's just punishment of His people for ignoring the laws. Together, they make an appeal for mercy to God. The second part of the book consists of two poems: one begs Israel to seek wisdom; the other, describing the terrible state of the city, looks forward to a better future.

Esdras

ESDRAS, GREEK FOR "EZRA," IS NOT CANONICAL
FOR CATHOLICS, PROTESTANTS, OR JEWS. THE
CATHOLIC AND ORTHODOX BIBLES EXPAND THE
BOOK OF ESTHER WITH SIX ADDITIONAL CHAPTERS.

Esdras is a Greco-Latin form of "Ezra." The first versions of the Bible do not distinguish between the Book of Ezra and the Book of Nehemiah, choosing instead to call them 1 Ezra and 2 Ezra, respectively. Though historians attribute Esdras to the prophet Ezra, it was actually written much later, during the first century CE. Not a part of the Catholic, Protestant, or Jewish canons, 2 Esdras forms part of the Apocrypha of the

> Until the land had enjoyed her sabbaths, the whole time of her desolation shall she rest, until the full term of seventy years.
>
> 1 ESDRAS 1:58

King James Bible. An apocalyptic book, 2 Esdras describes seven visions of the prophet, climaxing with a description of the glory of New Jerusalem. Though set at the time of the Babylonian destruction, 2 Esdras was likely written in reaction to the second razing of the temple in 70 CE.

King Esdras

ADDITIONS TO ESTHER

Esther meets with the king

THE CATHOLIC AND ORTHODOX BIBLES have six additional chapters in the Book of Esther, based on a Greek translation by Jerome in the late fourth century. The additions expand the story and include an opening dream by Mordecai, the full reading of the decree against the Jews, the decree in favor of the Jews, prayers to God by Mordecai and Esther, and Mordecai's interpretation of his dream.

1 and 2 Maccabees

THE MACCABEES REVOLT AGAINST KING ANTIOCHUS AND TAKE JERUSALEM, REESTABLISHING THE JEWISH TEMPLE. THE YEARLY FESTIVAL OF HANUKKAH CELEBRATES THIS VICTORY.

In the Orthodox and Roman Catholic canon, the two books of Maccabees offer an invaluable glimpse of the Jewish world just prior to the birth of Christ. The name *Maccabee*, which means "hammer-headed," comes from the heroic family that led a revolt for Jewish independence.

In 1 Maccabees we read a description of Alexander the Great's conquest of the Persians who ruled Jerusalem. The Seleucid king, Antiochus IV, conquers Egypt and Judah by 175 BCE, and in an attempt to Hellenize the region he outlaws Judaism, taking all the valuables out of the temple. Judas Maccabeus and his family initiate a revolt against the king.

Judas Maccabeus before the Army of Nicanor

They are eventually successful and they liberate the temple in 165 BCE. Judas asks for Rome's help in ridding the region of the Seleucids, inaugurating the festival of Hanukkah. When his brother, Simon, becomes high priest and, later, the prince of Israel, the Hasmonean Dynasty—a period of rule by kings not descended from David's bloodline—begins.

In 2 Maccabees we see a more theologically based explanation of events, including a promise of life after death for the Maccabean martyrs, a popular concept for Christians.

> In those days went there out of Israel wicked men, who persuaded many, saying, Let us go and make a covenant with the heathen that are round about us: for since we departed from them we have had much sorrow.
>
> MACCABEES 1:11

THE NEW TESTAMENT

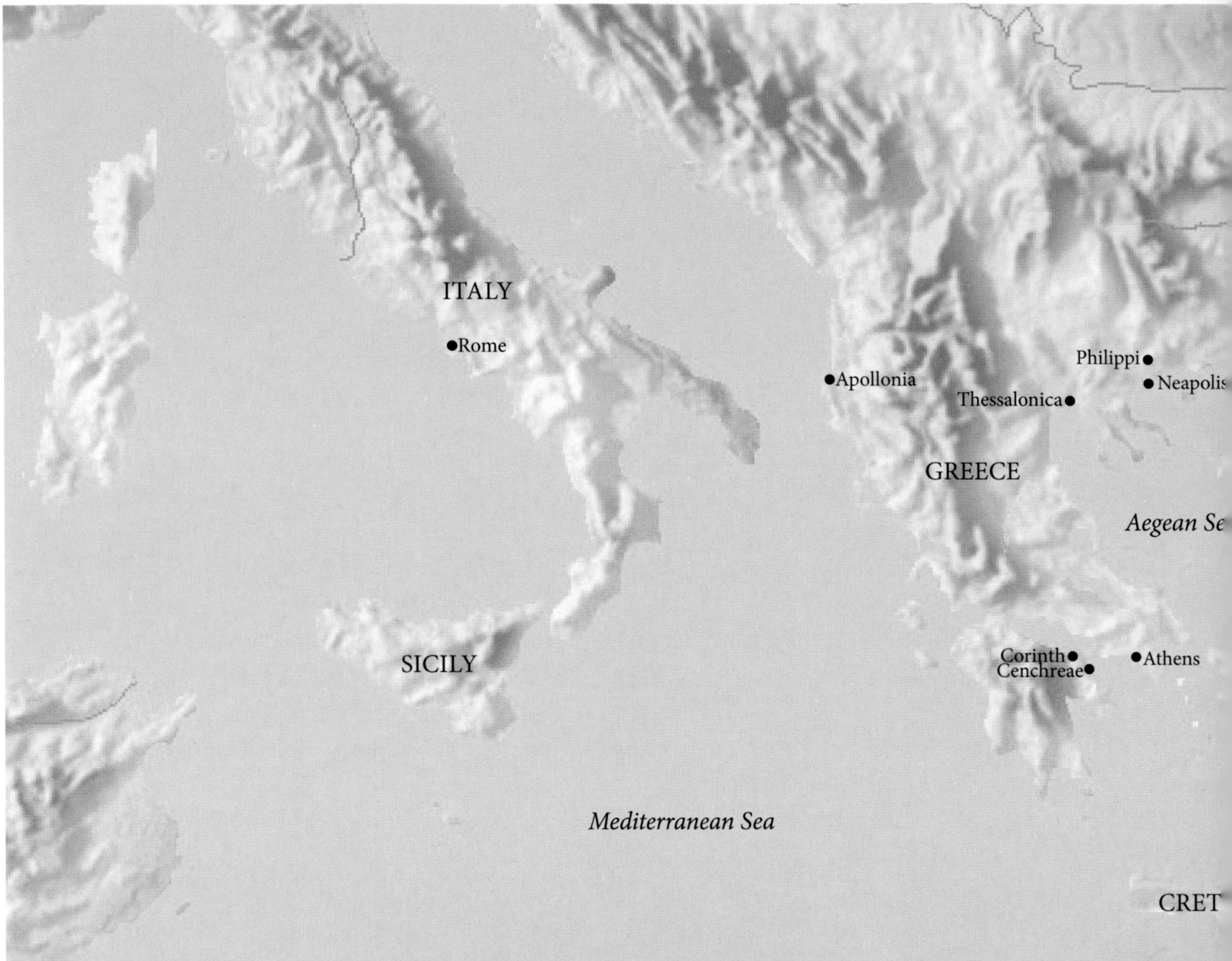

ITALY

●Rome

●Apollonia

Philippi●

Thessalonica● ●Neapolis

GREECE

Aegean Se

Corinth● ●Athens
Cenchreae●

SICILY

Mediterranean Sea

CRET

EASTERN
MEDITERRANEAN

From its beginnings in Palestine, where Jesus lived and died, Christianity spread into the surrounding lands. In the era in which the events of the New Testament took place, the eastern Mediterranean was under Roman rule, and the apostles used the empire's roads and ports to spread the word of the Gospel throughout the region and beyond.

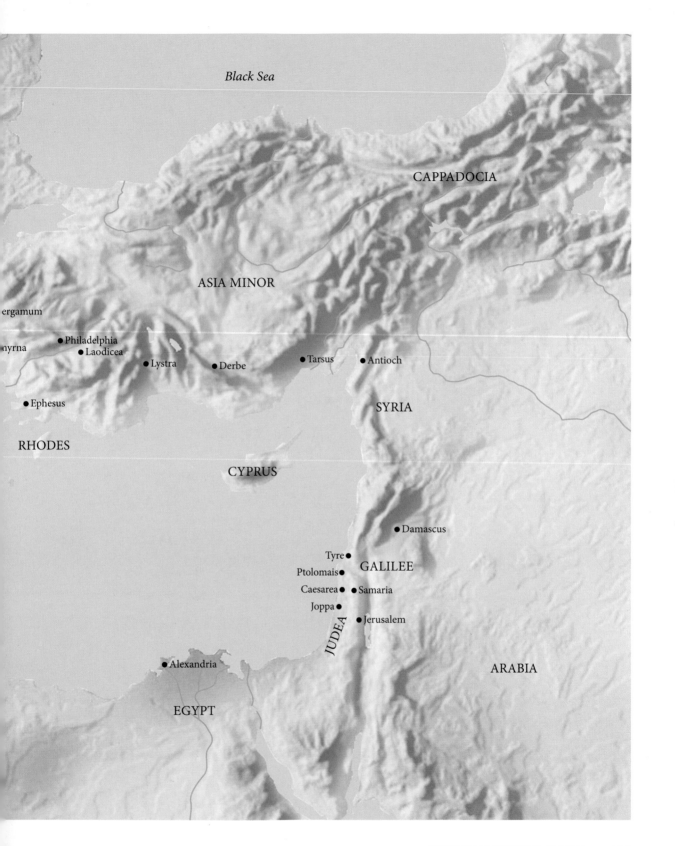

Black Sea

CAPPADOCIA

ASIA MINOR

ergamum

● Philadelphia
myrna ● Laodicea

● Lystra   ● Derbe   ● Tarsus   ● Antioch

● Ephesus

SYRIA

RHODES

CYPRUS

● Damascus

Tyre ●

Ptolomais ●   GALILEE

Caesarea ●   ● Samaria

Joppa ●

JUDEA   ● Jerusalem

● Alexandria   ARABIA

EGYPT

Life in the Time of Jesus

As a boy in Nazareth, Jesus lived under the dominion of Rome, practicing his religion and following the Law of Moses. Allowed freedom of religion and tradition, Jewish citizens fell under the jurisdiction of the Sanhedrin, a Jewish court. Yet, imperial authority still dominated over important decisions, such as determining the use of the death penalty.

With Israel's location on the Mediterranean, shipping was an important part of the economy, and the country exported olives, figs, grain, dates, and wine throughout the empire. Jews and Gentiles observed strict social divisions, especially among the more conservative Pharisees. Citizens resented the heavy tax burden Rome imposed, and Jews were also expected to tithe and provide sacrificial animals for the temple. The temple priests, the Sadducees, composed the upper class of society. Politically adept, they also managed to stay on better terms with their Roman rulers. The Pharisees, middle-class scribes, were merchants and artisans. They joined their lower-class brethren in awaiting the arrival of the promised Messiah, who would free them from Roman oppression and tyranny and restore Jewish autonomy to Israel.

The Presentation of Christ in the Temple

Christ in the Storm. Jesus grew up in the towns and villages around the Sea of Galilee

PALESTINE

In the first century CE, Palestine, or the Land
of Israel, was divided into three provinces:
Judea, Galilee, and Samaria. Jesus spent
time in the Judean Desert before launching
his ministry in earnest, mostly in the areas
around the Sea of Galilee.

Damascus ●

Tyre ●

GALILEE

Ptolomais ●

Capernaum ● ● Bethsaida

Sea of Galilee

Cana ●

Nazareth ●

Caesarea ●

SAMARIA

Mediterranean Sea

Joppa ●   ● Arimathaea

● Emmaus   ● Jericho

● Jerusalem
● Bethlehem

JUDEA

Dead Sea

Gaza ●

IDUMEA   Masada ●

ARABIA

SINAI

PREFECTS AND KINGS

In the years surrounding the events of the New Testament, the Roman Empire controlled Judea. To administer its vast territory, the Roman emperor appointed loyal supporters to govern and collect taxes in his name.

ROME RULED OVER PALESTINE beginning in 63 BCE, when General Pompey seized Jerusalem. Roman political appointments, made at the whim of Caesar, included supervised monarchical rule as well as so-called prefects. A prefect was an official of ancient Rome, devoted to the emperor and directly responsible to him, to maintain order during Jewish festivals, such as Passover. Pontius Pilate, who served from 26 to 36 CE, is the most famous of the prefects of Judea.

Although Herod the Great was named king of the Jews in 40 BCE, he did not gain control of his kingdom until 37 BCE. He was an able ruler, carrying out

Herod the Great, King of the Jews

For of a truth against thy holy child Jesus, whom thou hast anointed, both Herod, and Pontius Pilate, with the Gentiles, and the people of Israel, were gathered together.

ACTS 4:27

---

who managed the financial affairs of a province or acted as governor of a lesser province. Roman-appointed prefects governed in Judea concurrently with the reign of the Herodians (6 to 41 CE and 44 to 46 CE). They lived in Caesarea, the Roman capital of Judea, but stayed in Jerusalem

Rome's wishes (and authorizing the "massacre of the innocents") until 4 BCE, the year of his death (and likely the year of Jesus's birth). After Herod's death, Caesar divided the territory among his three sons, Archelaus, Antipas (responsible for beheading John the Baptist), and

Philip, who ruled the far north and was not involved in New Testament events.

Herod the Great's grandson, Herod Agrippa I, took over Philip's territory and eventually governed the rest of Palestine from 41 to 44 CE. After 35

Christ and Pilate—What Is Truth?

years under the Roman yoke, a Jewish king once again ruled Palestine—one who had thoroughly assimilated Roman values and numbered the Emperor Caligula among his many highly placed friends. Pro-Roman and Hellenistic in his tastes, Herod Agrippa I stamped his image on coins. Being hailed as a god at a festival of the cult of emperor worship, he collapsed in pain and died five days later, leading Jews to believe God had struck him down because he accepted praise as a deity.

Judea was once again subject to the control of Roman prefects until approximately 50 CE. Agrippa II retired in 70 CE, after the fall of Jerusalem; historians believe he died in Rome in 100 CE. It was Agrippa II who heard the Apostle Paul's case.

Judaism

JUDAISM TRACES ITS ROOTS BACK THREE THOUSAND YEARS TO THE TIME OF ABRAHAM. BOTH A RELIGION AND A CULTURAL IDENTITY, THE THREE MAJOR DIVISIONS OF MODERN JUDAISM THRIVE AROUND THE WORLD.

The Book of Esther, which takes place in the late fifth century BCE, is the first Biblical book to use the word "Jewish" to identify a member of a Hebrew tribe. The word *Judaism* itself derives from the tribe and country of Judah, to which the Hebrews who had scattered return following the Babylonian exile.

Judaism is one of the world's oldest monotheistic religions, and the origins of the Jewish faith can be traced back three thousand years, to the time God makes His covenant with Abraham. Uniquely, Judaism also signifies its adherents' ethnic and cultural background. Unlike the polytheist deities of their neighbors, the Hebrew God is especially concerned with humankind and the

When Esther becomes queen, Ahasuerus does not know she is Jewish

natural world. God expects His children to follow His example of love and respect for everything He has created; in return for honoring Him as their sole deity, God promises the Jews that they will become a great nation in the land that He has given them.

Though beliefs vary within Judaism, with some Jews observing stricter religious laws, all follow the Law as Moses lays out. Jews universally honor the covenant with Abraham and recognize the basic principles of the Hebrew Bible. Because Jews consider "Jewishness" a tribal identity, they do not seek out converts—and whether religious or nonreligious, the faith considers one Jewish if born to a Jewish mother.

After Alexander the Great conquered the region in 332 BCE, many Jews begin adopting Hellenic ways, and Greek became the official language of commerce. With the installation of the non-Davidic Hasmonean Dynasty in the second century BCE, King Jonathan encouraged Jewish conversions in conquered neighboring territories, and when the Romans came, these foreign occupiers appointed Jewish rulers and temple high priests. Though he lacked Jewish blood, Herod the Great, an Idumean convert, inaugurated a dynasty of kings ruling the Jewish state. The temple in

Prayer of Moses before Israelites passed through the Red Sea

Jerusalem was the center of Jewish religious worship until the Romans destroyed it in 70 CE; a court, known as the Sanhedrin, administered religious laws and settled disputes. With the obliteration of these focal points of Jewish worship and culture, and the second siege of Jerusalem by the Romans, Jewish religious practices became less centralized as adherents scattered throughout the world.

Jewish Groups

BY THE FIRST CENTURY CE, THERE WERE AT LEAST 24 DIFFERENT JEWISH SECTS PRACTICING IN JUDEA ALONGSIDE CHRISTIANITY, WHICH BEGAN TO DEVELOP AFTER THE DEATH OF JESUS CHRIST.

Chafing under Roman occupation, many of the at least 24 sects practicing in Judea in the first century looked to the arrival of a messiah, a military as well as religious leader, who would rise up and throw off the yoke of foreign rule once and for all. The Pharisees, Sadducees, Essenes, and Zealots were the most influential of these groups.

The Pharisees, the largest of the four, were also the most xenophobic, abjuring whenever possible interactions with foreigners. Many other Jews considered them self-righteous, but the Pharisees took their religious practices most seriously.

Jesus silences the Pharisees and Sadducees

In contrast, the Sadducees were open to studying outside cultures; appointed by civil officials, they were politically connected and astute. The Sadducees, who also controlled the priesthood, held as crucially important the first five books of the Old Testament.

The Essene community, the most spiritual of the four, lived monastically, believing devoutly in a coming messianic kingdom.

The Zealots—highly political, revolutionary messianists who believed in violence as a means of overthrowing their oppressors—actually frightened their Roman rulers.

Feast of Simon the Pharisee

The Temple

KING HEROD BUILT HIS TEMPLE IN JERUSALEM ON THE ORIGINAL SITE OF SOLOMON'S. MUCH LARGER AND GRANDER THAN THE ORIGINAL STRUCTURE, THE NEW TEMPLE INSPIRED AWE IN JEWS AND CHRISTIANS ALIKE.

From the time of King David, the idea of a great temple in Jerusalem, a place to commune with God, played a significant role in the lives of the Jewish people. The Jews rebuilt the second temple in 516 BCE, after the Babylonian exile. It would endure desecration under several foreign occupations until its rededication following the Maccabean revolt. Not until 19 BCE, under the leadership of Herod I, did it achieve its full glory. It was Herod's dream to be remembered

Reconstruction of Jerusalem and the Temple of Herod

for the creation of one of the most magnificent buildings in the world. Choosing the temple in his home city of Jerusalem, he greatly expanded the ancient be seen for miles, became the gleaming focal point of the city. Pilgrims and sightseers thronged the site, and money changers, tour guides, and souvenir sellers

---

Is it time for you, O ye, to dwell in your cieled houses, and this house *lie* waste?

HAGGAI 1:4

Expulsion of the Money Changers from the Temple

site, hiring architects from Greece, Rome, and Egypt.

Workers completed the bulk of construction in three years. The final result was so magnificent that the temple, which could filled the Court of the Gentiles. Inside halls were reserved for Jews and priests performing animal sacrifices. In 70 CE, Rome destroyed Herod's temple during the First Jewish War.

THE DEAD SEA SCROLLS

One of the greatest historical and scholarly discoveries of the twentieth century
was uncovered in a cliff cave near the Dead Sea. Although time had worn the scrolls
to pieces, scholars are still reassembling the fragments to find parts
of the Old and New Testaments, and many nonbiblical Jewish writings.

Portion of a photographic reproduction of the Great Isaiah Scroll

IN 1947, A BEDOUIN BOY, looking for a lost goat, stumbled upon a cave, which turned out to contain some ancient Hebrew scrolls. Further investigation at the site, 13 miles east of Jerusalem near the ruins of Qumrum, revealed that an ancient Jewish library had been hidden in the caves, possibly for protection against the Roman army at the time of the First Jewish Revolt (66–70 CE). By any measure an astonishingly important biblical-archeological treasure trove, the Dead Sea Scrolls reveal the roots of early Christianity in Judaism, providing insight into the times of Jesus without ever mentioning Him or the new Christian sect directly. Their discovery (1947–56) still reverberates today, despite the fact that translations of many of the scrolls have yet to be released.

The scrolls were likely written by the Essenes—spiritual

ascetics who devoted themselves to God by faithfully copying the Old Testament in their scriptorium—between 200 BCE and 68 CE. Most are in Hebrew, but there are many in Aramaic and a few in Greek. Written in carbon-based ink on animal skin and papyrus, with no spaces between words, the scrolls were stored in tall clay jars.

Prior to their discovery, the oldest known versions of the Old Testament in Hebrew dated

Portion of the Temple Scroll, one of the longest of the Dead Sea Scrolls

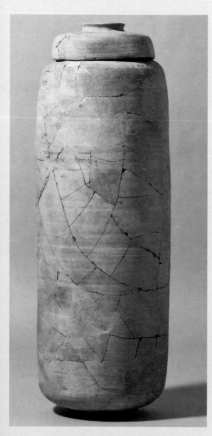

Dead Sea Scroll jar

to 920 CE; one copy, made in 1008 CE, was used in 1611 CE to create the King James Bible. Yet, to the amazement of historians, the copy of the Old Testament found among the Dead Sea Scrolls matches this later version almost word for word, despite the fact that it predates it by one thousand years. Scholars have also identified an Isaiah Scroll, dating to 200 BCE, that is one thousand years older than any previously known copy of Isaiah.

Along with a copy of the complete Old Testament (with the exception of the Book of Esther), findings at the site include additional prophecies of Ezekiel, Jeremiah, and Daniel, further psalms attributed to King David and Joshua, which are not contained in the Bible, and new stories about Noah, Enoch, and Abraham—including an explanation of God's request that Abraham sacrifice his son Isaac. The last words of Joseph, Judah, Levi, Naphtali, and Amram (father of Moses) have also been unearthed.

The First Jewish War

WITH JERUSALEM UNDER ROMAN OCCUPATION, THE JEWS IGNITED
A MASS PROTEST AGAINST HIGH TAXES. TENSIONS ESCALATED,
RESULTING IN MANY DEATHS AND THE DESTRUCTION OF THE GREAT CITY.

Long-simmering resentment of the Roman occupation of Judea and Jerusalem erupted in 66 CE, when Roman troops allowed Greeks to sacrifice birds in front of a synagogue. In retaliation, the high priest stopped saying prayers for the Roman emperor. Roman citizens and Jews perceived to be traitors were harassed on the streets.

Eventually, the people staged massive protests against Roman taxation, and the pro-Roman king fled. When, in 66 CE, the Romans attempted to restore order by sending troops, Jewish militia slaughtered six thousand of them at the Battle of Beth Horon. Shocked and dismayed, Rome sent General Vespasian and his son, Titus, to crush the rebellion. Working their way through the countryside, the victorious Roman legions eventually reached Jerusalem, the center of the rebellion.

The walls of Jerusalem had been under siege for some time before the Romans breached them in the summer of 70 CE. Anyone caught fleeing the city was crucified. The Sicarii Zealots, refusing to allow surrender, set fire to the dried food supply. By the time the Romans entered the city, no fewer than 600,000 Jews had either been slaughtered or starved to death. The city of Jerusalem and its temple were completely destroyed.

The Spoils of War (Arch of Titus)

Titus destroying Jerusalem

Masada

THOUGH THE BIBLE DOES NOT MENTION MASADA BY NAME,
IT HAD TIES TO THE NEW TESTAMENT. KING HEROD I DEVELOPED THIS CITY,
AMONG OTHERS, AS A FORTRESS AND POINT OF ESCAPE FROM ENEMIES.

The Siege of Masada

The word *masada* means "fortress." An outcropping of palaces, barracks, and fortifications on the edge of the Judean Desert, high over the Dead Sea was the spot Herod I chose to build Masada. It was intended as a refuge in case of civil insurrection during his reign in the last century BCE. Almost one hundred years later, in 73 CE, it became the site of the final siege of the First Jewish War.

After fleeing the destroyed city of Jerusalem, the remaining Sicarii Zealots, joined by other families, encamped at the isolated fortress. The Romans, believing it crucial to destroy the Zealots, laid siege. Surrounding Masada, the Roman army moved thousands of tons of rock and earth, succeeding after several months in breaking down the wall with a battering ram. On entering the town, the troops found that nearly all of the 960 residents had committed suicide. Every building, apart from the one holding food, had been set ablaze. According to the historian Flavius Josephus, two women and five children, the sole survivors of the siege, reported that the storehouse had been left standing to prove that the people did not starve—they had chosen to die rather than be enslaved by Rome.

The ruins of Masada

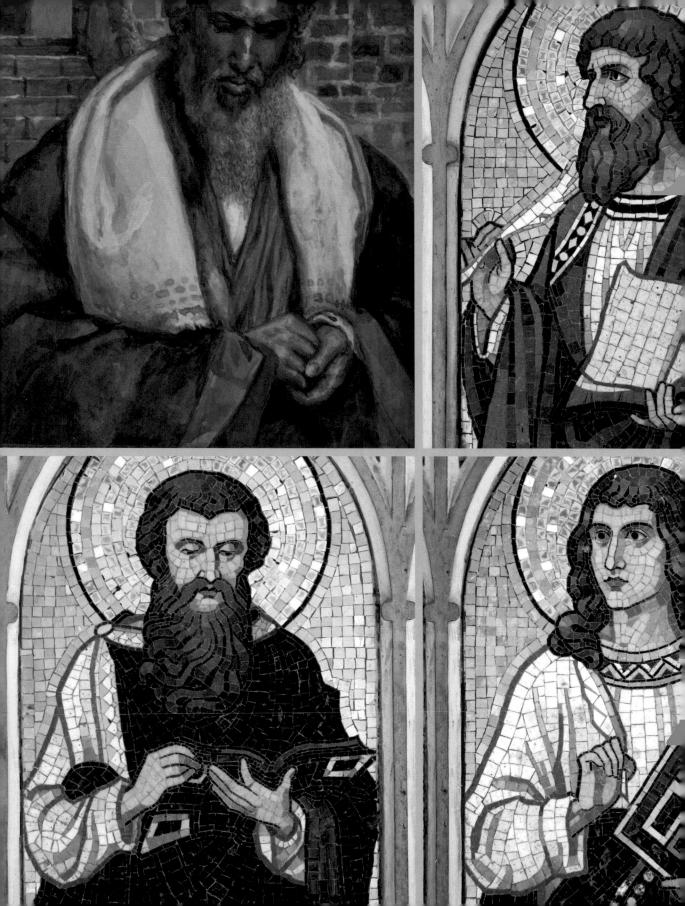

The
Gospels

The word *gospel* derives from the old English *god-spell*, meaning "good news," and Christians really do consider the accounts of Jesus's life to be good news, in that they tell the story of the savior of humanity. In the New Testament, there are four canonical gospels: Matthew, Mark, Luke, and John. Said to be written no later than the first century CE by men who interacted directly with Christ (or by His immediate followers), the Gospels tell the story of the birth, life, religious mission, death, and resurrection of Jesus. The texts, drawn from the oral tradition and from memory, have been put into writing in order to spread Christ's story to followers in different countries; as a result, Matthew, Mark, Luke, and John are known as the Four Evangelists. The first Christians followed many different gospels, but because they were written in later times, the early Church leaders elected not to include them in the New Testament canon.

Matthew, Mark, and Luke each relate Christ's biography from unique viewpoints, but John's gospel stands apart, portraying Jesus as the physical incarnation of God's word and explaining His relationship to God the Father and the Holy Spirit.

Mosaics of the Four Evangelists
CLOCKWISE FROM TOP LEFT: Saint Matthew, Saint Mark, Saint John, Saint Luke

THE SYNOPTIC GOSPELS

The first three books of the New Testament—Matthew, Mark, and Luke—are the primary sources of historical details about the life of Jesus Christ.

TOGETHER, THE FIRST THREE books of the New Testament are also known as the Synoptic Gospels. The name comes from the Greek words *syn*, meaning "together," and *optic*, meaning "seen" (or *opsis*, "appearance"), because the three can be compared column by column, as scholars frequently do when looking for historical facts about the life of Jesus or discerning intent when the accounts differ from one another. In general, the three books (all three possibly derived from a fourth source) agree about the key events in Jesus's life. Almost all of Mark's content is found in Matthew, and much of Mark is similarly found in Luke. Matthew and Luke, additionally, have a large amount of material in common that is not found in Mark.

The Synoptic Gospels were likely written between 70 to 90 CE, at a time when Nero was persecuting Christians and the Roman army was destroying Zealot Jews in Palestine. Paul was in prison, and eyewitnesses to Christ's ministry and miracles were dying off. How the gospels actually came to be may never be known, but believers hold dear the notion that God sent the Holy Spirit to three men

Saint Mark

Saint Luke

the three gospels, Mark's speaks to a Gentile audience, and, as such, it does not presume a vast knowledge of the Old Testament.

Placed third, Luke's more elaborate gospel embellishes Mark's outline, illustrating the concept of true piety through his inclusion of parables. As the only Gentile gospel writer, Luke does not focus on the fulfillment of prophecy, as Matthew does—he wants his readers to know that Christ can be savior of all people.

of differing backgrounds, in different places, all of whom recorded significantly similar lives of Christ and produced documents that have invigorated the Church for generations.

Matthew's gospel—which bridges the Old and New Testaments, frequently quoting the ancient prophets as proof that Jesus is the Messiah and fulfillment of the Davidic Covenant for Israel—appears first. Matthew is speaking directly to a Jewish audience.

Historians believe Mark's gospel, though placed second, was composed first and is based on the Apostle Peter's personal recollections. The shortest of

The Evangelist Matthew inspired by an Angel

SAINT MATTHEW

THE GOSPEL ACCORDING TO SAINT MATTHEW RECOUNTS THE LIFE OF JESUS, TRACING HIS ANCESTRY BACK TO ABRAHAM. MATTHEW QUOTES THE OLD TESTAMENT TO PROVE THAT CHRIST IS THE MESSIAH OF ANCIENT PROPHECIES.

Most readers consider the Gospel According to Matthew— written for a Hebrew audience and quoting the Old Testament more than 65 times—the most Jewish of the gospels. It is also the first book in the New Testament, forming a perfect bridge between the promises of the Old Testament and Matthew's proof, through scripture, that Christ is indeed the fulfillment of the promise of a coming Messiah.

The Calling of Saint Matthew

Matthew traces the ancestry of Jesus through David back to Abraham. He recounts the virgin birth of Christ, citing Isaiah, the slaughter of the innocents perpetrated by Herod I, the family's escape to Egypt, and their safe return

And Jesus came and spake unto them, saying, All power is given unto me in heaven and in earth. Go ye therefore, and teach all nations, baptizing them in the name of the Father, and of the Son, and of the Holy Ghost

MATTHEW 28:18–19

upon the king's death. Jesus is baptized and declared the son of God, retiring to the desert to fast and pray for forty days before beginning his mission.

Matthew's description of Jesus's mission in Galilee contains many

Baptism of Christ

parables and depictions of miracles. He stresses respect for the lowest members of the social order and describes frequent clashes with the Pharisees, who uphold the status quo in Jewish society. An outcast himself, Matthew is a tax collector—a despised though amply compensated career in the first century CE. Tax collectors worked for the Roman Empire, pocketing a portion of whatever they collected, and their fellow Jews considered them traitors.

When Jesus summons the Twelve apostles, all undistinguished, humble men—fishermen, workers, a revolutionary—Matthew gets up and follows him immediately. When the local Pharisees castigate Jesus for dining with a group of such disreputable men, Jesus answers that he has come to call on the pariahs, not the respectable people.

Matthew's Jesus challenges laws that impede His mission to heal, preach, and extend mercy. He details Christ's last week of life—His predictions, fears, and, finally, His conquest over death. The book ends with the risen Christ ordering His disciples out into the world to evangelize.

Written for an uprooted community after the destruction of the second temple, scholars believe that Matthew, as a Christian Jew, is arguing with the dogmatic scribes and Pharisees who do not recognize Christ as Messiah. Vested as they are in the concept of a savior-as-warrior king who would come to free them, they accord little respect to the redeemer who comes preaching love.

Saint Matthew

THE GOSPEL ACCORDING TO
SAINT MARK

MARK'S GOSPEL, THE OLDEST AND SHORTEST OF THE FOUR,
PERHAPS SERVED AS AN OUTLINE FOR MATTHEW AND LUKE'S
MORE ELABORATE ACCOUNTS OF CHRIST'S LIFE AND WORK.

Mark was the secretary to Saint Peter, Christ's first apostle. Tradition has it that Peter dictated his memories of Christ to Mark while Peter was imprisoned in Rome. The rushed, somewhat terse style of this gospel may well be a result of Peter's attempting to relate as much as possible prior to his execution.

Though Mark was likely Jewish, his gospel is aimed at Greek-speaking

Saint Peter preaching
in the presence
of Saint Mark

Gentiles. Opening with a reference from Isaiah to the "voice of one crying in the wilderness," which will pave the way for the Messiah, we are introduced to Jesus as He is baptized, and learn of His fast in the desert, His selection of the apostles, His healings and miracles, and His frequent disagreements with the Pharisees.

The primary focus of Mark's gospel is the last week of Christ's life and the suffering He must endure to atone for the sins of humanity. Mark observes a similarity in the executions of John the Baptist and Jesus: both men die as a result of rulers who are motivated by political expediency, rather than a desire for simple justice.

Mark describes the morning after Jesus's crucifixion and entombment. On their way to anoint his body, Mary Magdalene and two other women worry that they will not be able to roll away the stone sealing the tomb. To their amazement, however, the stone has already been rolled back, and the tomb is open. Inside they find a young man in white—Jesus of Nazareth—who tells them not to be afraid: he has been

Jesus and Mary Magdalene

raised from the dead. In Mark's original rendering, Jesus asks the women to inform Peter that He has risen, but instead they run away in fright. In later versions, which depict the resurrection from the viewpoints of the three other evangelists, Jesus appears to Mary Magdalene and then to His disciples before ascending into heaven to be united with God for all eternity.

THE GOSPEL ACCORDING TO
SAINT LUKE

LUKE IS THE ONLY GENTILE AUTHOR OF THE NEW TESTAMENT. AS A FOLLOWER OF SAINT PAUL, LUKE IS NOT PRESENT AT THE INCARNATION.

A physician with an excellent vocabulary, Luke writes his gospel from Greece as a letter to Theophilus (Paul's defense attorney while he is on trial in Rome, though others believe he is Luke's publisher).

Saint Luke drawing a portrait of the Virgin Mary

Luke spends years interviewing witnesses and accumulating texts in an attempt to compile a historically accurate account of the events surrounding the life of Christ. With its ringing emphasis on Christ's humanity, the Gospel of Luke is, by far, the most joyous and detailed of the gospels. Luke, who is not as interested in proving the fulfillment of prophecy,

---

And all flesh shall see the salvation of God."

LUKE 3:6

---

quotes the Old Testament only when needed, and although he traces Jesus's genealogy all the way back to Adam, he does so more to prove Christ's universal humanity than to assure his place in the Jewish pantheon.

This book depicts Jesus as praying before every major event in His life, and Luke employs more prayer and praise than the other gospel writers, including the Magnificat of Mary, Zechariah's prophecy, the praise of the shepherds

Parable of the Good Samaritan

and angels, and the blessings of the high priest Simeon. Luke also includes the well-known parables of the Good Samaritan and the Prodigal Son. A major emphasis in the book, which also portrays women playing major roles in Jesus's ministry, is the accessibility of His good news to everyone, especially the downtrodden.

Luke presents the trial of Jesus, His execution, and His death in a calm, manner, making the events appear inevitable. In this retelling, the political demands of the Jewish hierarchy, rather than the perfidy of Pontius Pilate, are responsible for Christ's execution. (Portraying the death of Jesus in this light is, many believe, Luke's attempt at assuaging the Roman Empire's growing suspicions of Christian loyalty.) On rising from the dead, Jesus joins some followers on the walk to Emmaus and has a meal with them before vanishing. He next visits His disciples, promising to send the Holy Spirit to them. Extending His hand in blessing, He ascends into heaven and is gone.

THE GOSPEL ACCORDING TO
SAINT JOHN

THE GOSPEL ACCORDING TO SAINT JOHN INTRODUCES THE BIBLICAL CONCEPT OF THE WORD, EVOLVED FROM THE GREEK CONCEPT OF "LOGOS," OR REASON. JOHN FOCUSES ON JESUS'S LAST DAYS AND HIS RESURRECTION.

Referring to Jesus as "the Word," the Gospel According to Saint John introduces the divine Jesus in its first few lines. The Word, John says, was there at the beginning; through the Word, the source of light that shines even in darkness, God created all things. The Word became human, living in grace and truth; likewise, those who recognize and follow the Word become children of God. The Greeks referred to the mysterious cosmic energy that powered creation as the *logos*, meaning "word" or "reason," and the Old Testament says God spoke all things into being. In his attempt to explain Jesus's divinity, John, scholars

believe, seized on the idea, novel for his time, of combining these two concepts.

John's is not one of the Synoptic Gospels (he omits parables, most miracles, and the Sermon on the Mount). Composed at the end of the first century CE the book, purportedly written by Jesus's favorite apostle as

> Jesus saith unto him, I am the way, the truth, and the life: no man cometh unto the Father, but by me.
>
> JOHN 14:6

an elderly man, notably relates, among other differences, Jesus's four years of public ministry to the other gospels' one. John describes the last week of Jesus's life and the resurrection after His death, quoting Jesus, who is washing His disciples' feet at the Last Supper: "Verily, verily, I say unto you, the servant is not greater than his lord; neither he that is sent greater than he that sent him. If ye know these

The Wedding at Cana

Resurrection of Christ and Women at the Tomb

things, happy are ye if ye do them" (John 13:16–17). He details Jesus's relationship with His followers on the night of His arrest and His charge to Peter to care for the others. The only gospel to mention the Wedding at Cana, where Jesus turns water into wine, John's is also the only gospel to depict the raising of Lazarus from the dead.

Many believe that John, who describes seven miracles performed by Jesus, chose to write about them primarily for their symbolic significance. In his attempt to explain the basic tenets of Christianity—how Jesus, a man, is also God incarnate—John uses simple symbols to explain profound concepts, describing Jesus variously as the lamb of God, the bread of life, the light of the world, the good shepherd, the way, the truth, and the life, and the true grapevine.

Mary, Mother of Jesus

CHRISTIANS DIFFER IN THEIR VIEWS ON THE RELIGIOUS IMPORTANCE OF MARY, MOTHER OF JESUS CHRIST. FOR CATHOLICS, ESPECIALLY, SHE IS A REVERED AND CENTRAL FIGURE DESPITE HER RELATIVE ABSENCE FROM MANY PASSAGES IN THE NEW TESTAMENT.

Perhaps nothing illustrates the division between Christian sects more vividly than the treatment accorded to Mary, Mother of Jesus. Mentioned only twenty times in the Bible, most Protestants view her as only minimally important. Roman and Elisabeth, greets her similarly, Mary recites the Magnificat, a beautiful song of praise for God. In fulfillment of the prediction Isaiah made seven hundred years earlier, Mary is the virgin who conceives and gives birth to a son known as Immanuel, or "God is with us."

pilgrimage to Jerusalem. When, days later, she finds him in the temple debating His elders, he asks her, "How is it that ye sought me? Wist ye not that I must be about my Father's business?" (Luke 2:49). Jesus performs His first miracle at Mary's behest, turning water into wine at the

And Mary said, My soul doth magnify the Lord, And my spirit hath rejoiced in God my Savior. For he hath regarded the low estate of his handmaiden: for, behold, from henceforth all generations shall call me blessed.

LUKE 1:46–48

Orthodox Catholics, on the other hand, as well as Lutherans and Anglicans, have granted her the title Theotokos, "Birth-giver of God" or "Mother of God."

Mary is most often mentioned in the Gospel According to Saint Luke. As a young woman engaged to marry Joseph, the Angel Gabriel visits her and tells her she is to be the mother of the coming Messiah, conceived by the Holy Spirit. Though troubled, Mary accepts. When her cousin,

When Mary and Joseph present Jesus at the temple and make their sacrificial offering, the holy man Simeon praises the baby, blessing his parents, but gives Mary a warning: because Jesus will have so much division around him, "Yea, a sword shall pierce through thy own soul also . . ." (Luke 2:35). Later, Mary is a frantic mother looking for the 12-year-old Jesus when He is separated from His parents returning from the Passover

Wedding at Cana, and the Gospel According to Saint John places Mary at the foot of the cross, mourning while Jesus is dying. Christ asks His most beloved disciple to attend to His mother after His death.

Mary receives one final mention in the Bible: with the eleven remaining disciples, she prays after Jesus's ascension into heaven.

The Virgin with Angels

The Nativity

OF THE FOUR GOSPEL WRITERS, ONLY MATTHEW AND LUKE DISCUSS THE NATIVITY. BOTH CITE BETHLEHEM AS THE BIRTHPLACE OF JESUS, THEREBY FULFILLING MICAH'S CENTURIES-OLD PROPHECY.

According to Luke, shortly before the birth of Jesus, when the ruling Romans announce that everyone must return to their home cities for a census, Joseph and a very pregnant Mary leave Nazareth, eventually arriving in Bethlehem. Unable to find a room there, Mary delivers her baby in an inn's stable. Angels appear to shepherds in a field, announcing that Jesus, the savior, has just been born; the shepherds rush to the stable to honor and adore the infant in the manger.

A week later, Joseph and Mary have the infant circumcised: as a firstborn son, He is to be dedicated to the Lord as prescribed by Moses.

The Nativity

> And she brought forth her firstborn son, and wrapped him in swaddling clothes, and laid him in a manger; because there was no room for them in the inn.
>
> LUKE 2:7

Joseph and Mary then take Jesus to the temple in Jerusalem. There a man named Simeon, deeply moved by the Holy Spirit, takes the baby in his arms, giving thanks to God for fulfilling his promise to send a savior to earth. Amazed by the holy man's predictions, Joseph and Mary return to Nazareth in Galilee to raise the baby.

Matthew's version, the shorter of the two nativity stories, describes Jesus's birth through the premonitions of three wise visitors from the East. The magi, Gaspar, Melchior, and Balthasar, realizing that the king of the Jews has been born, decide to pay tribute. They find Jesus by following the Star of Bethlehem.

In Jerusalem, meanwhile, Herod is extremely upset upon receiving news of the birth.

> For unto you is born this day in the city of David a Savior, which is Christ the Lord.
>
> LUKE 2:11

"Where," he asks the chief priests, "is the Messiah to be born?" "In Bethlehem," they tell him, quoting Micah 5:2. Herod decrees that every male child in Bethlehem under the age of two is to be slaughtered, so that no future king will ever rival him. The resulting carnage mirrors the slaughter of Egypt's sons in Moses's time. An angel orders Joseph to uproot his family and flee to Egypt. They leave following Herod's death, settling in the province of Galilee in Nazareth, which Joseph feels will be safer than Judea.

The Star of Bethlehem guided the Three Wise Men to the Stable.

The Adoration of the Shepherds

John the Baptist

JOHN THE BAPTIST IS BORN TO ELISABETH, AN OLDER COUSIN OF MARY, MAKING HIM JESUS'S RELATIVE. JOHN HOLDS A SPECIAL PLACE IN CHRISTIANITY AS CHRIST'S MESSENGER.

Saint John the Baptist in the Wilderness

Known as "the forerunner," or messenger who will announce the coming of the Messiah, John the Baptist, dressed in camel skins and living as a hermit, is like an Old Testament prophet bridging the world of the ancient Hebrews and the new Christian faith.

According to Luke, John's conception is almost as auspicious as that of his cousin Jesus. His father, Zacharias, is an older priest in the temple when the Archangel Gabriel appears, informing him that his wife Elisabeth will soon have a son. Zacharias, questioning this possibility, is struck dumb. On returning home, however, he finds that Elisabeth is, indeed, expecting. Elisabeth names her son John, but when the neighbors insist that she name him for his father, Zacharias, still mute, writes on a tablet "his name is John," and instantly recovers his voice. He prophesies that John will pave the way for the coming Messiah.

John becomes a popular preacher as he grows up, subsisting on locusts and honey and living ascetically. People flock to his hermitage along the Jordan River, where they confess their sins and purify themselves by being baptized in its water. John preaches the necessity of repentance, for indeed, the kingdom of heaven is at hand.

Jesus arrives to be baptized, and John recognizes his kinsman as the Messiah about whom he has been preaching. As John baptizes Him, the Holy Spirit descends in the form of a dove, and several of John's followers become Jesus's first disciples.

Later, John, who had publicly rebuked Herod Antipas for marrying his brother's wife,

Angel appearing to Zacharias

Herodias, is imprisoned. Herodias's daughter Salome dances for the king, so pleasing him that he promises her anything in the world. At the celebrate June 24 as his feast day, near the summer solstice. In the Gospel of John, when John is questioned about the growing popularity of Jesus, he says,

> And she, before being instructed of her mother, said, Give me here John Baptist's head in a charger.
>
> MATTHEW 14:8

prompting of her mother, she asks for John's head on a plate, a request with which Herod Antipas reluctantly complies.

John was six months older than Jesus, so Christians "He must increase, while I must decrease." Daylight decreases at the summer solstice, just as it increases at the winter solstice, near December 25, the Feast of the Nativity of Jesus.

Salome carrying the head of John the Baptist on a platter

The Baptism of Christ

The Parables

FAVORED BY JESUS, PARABLES USE COMPARISONS TO TEACH MORAL LESSONS. IN BIBLICAL TIMES, THEY WERE COMMON TEACHING TOOLS IN THE MIDDLE EAST, AND THE NEW TESTAMENT CONTAINS MANY.

The Synoptic Gospels are filled with Jesus's teaching parables, which utilize common everyday situations to explain complex spiritual truths containing the central tenets of Christianity. The essence of what Jesus is trying to explain in these brief stories remains long after He has engaged and entertained His listeners with them.

Christians still contemplate, teach, and debate Jesus's parables today. So many of their elements have significance, regardless of the listener's culture or religion: seeds, earth, vineyards, yeast, houses, weeds, crops, food, nets, jewels,

> Then shall the kingdom of heaven be likened unto ten virgins, which took their lamps, and went forth to meet the bridegroom.
>
> MATTHEW 25:1

animals, money, family relations, the rich and poor—much of these things have remained unchanged for more than two thousand years, and Jesus's gift for using them metaphorically remains without parallel.

In explaining the Final Judgment, for example, Jesus relates the parable of the Drawing in the Net, in which fishermen throw a net into a lake and pull up every kind of fish. When they get to shore, they put the good fish into buckets and throw the rest away. Similarly, Jesus says, at the end of the age the angels will come and divide the evil from the good, keeping the good and throwing the evil into a fiery furnace.

The parable of the Unforgiving Servant relates the importance of forgiveness: a king, checking on his accounts, discovers that a servant owes him a large amount of money, which he is unable to pay back. When the servant begs

The Parable of the Rich Fool

for more time, the king forgives the debt. Later, when he finds the servant harassing a man who owes him money, the king has the servant thrown in jail for not showing others the mercy the king showed him. "This is how my father in Heaven will treat every one of you unless you forgive your brother from your heart," Jesus concludes.

When Matthew asks Jesus why He always teaches in parables, Jesus says He is trying to explain the secrets of the kingdom of Heaven. Though they might seem very obvious to some, there are those who, "seeing they may see, and not perceive; and hearing they may hear, and not understand" (Mark 4:12).

Kitchen Interior with the Parable of the Rich Man and the Poor Lazarus

Parable of the Wise and Foolish Virgins (also known as the Ten Virgins)

GALILEE

In the time of Jesus, Israel was divided into three provinces: Judea, Samaria, and the largest, Galilee. Galilee was the region of northern Israel that included Nazareth, the town where Jesus lived for the first thirty years of his life, and Capernaum, where his early ministry takes place.

GALILEE HAS A PRESENCE in both the Old and New Testaments. Solomon gives twenty cities in Galilee to Hiram, king of Tyre, as partial payment for the materials and workers he supplies for the building of the Temple. Prophet Jonah comes from Gath-hepher (a few miles north of Nazareth); prophet Elijah comes from Thisbe, in Upper Galilee.

The people of the towns scattered in the hills and on the shores of the lake are ethnically mixed. About 50 percent are Jews, like Joseph and his family, who speak Aramaic; the remainder mainly speak Greek. Galileans were hardworking people, who often come up against the Romans and developed a reputation as

> And came down to Capernaum, a city of Galilee, and taught them on the sabbath days.
>
> LUKE 4:31

dissidents for resisting Herod's rule. The region had a long history of turmoil, and political and economic protests and tax revolts against Rome were not uncommon. The Maccabees seized Galilee from the Syrians around 130 BCE. Rome, in turn, defeated the Maccabees in 63 BCE, returning much of the territory

Jesus Stilling the Tempest

The Miraculous Draught of Fishes

to Syria, then also under the control of Rome.

Surrounded by mountains, the area was lush with trees and fertile fields and contained the Sea of Galilee, a fish-filled, freshwater lake fed from the north by the Jordan River, which continued south to the Dead Sea. There, Jesus preached and performed the miracles of walking on water and feeding the five thousand. Jesus recruited the fishermen—James, John, and Peter—from this lake to be his disciples. Jesus preached and related many of His parables in the province of Galilee, and He performed 25 of His recorded miracles there, including His first (wine in Cana) and His last (healing Malchus's ear).

The Gospel According to Saint John (21:1–14) tells the story of how, after the Resurrection, some of the disciples, returning to their work as fishermen, catch nothing. Jesus stands, unrecognized, on the shore of the Sea of Galilee. He then tells them to cast their net again, this time from the right side of the boat.

When they cast the net as He instructed, it fills with fish, and the disciples know they are in the presence of their lord.

Christ and the Centurion of Capernaum

Miracles

THE GOSPELS CONTAIN NUMEROUS MIRACLE STORIES IN WHICH JESUS EXERTS MIRACULOUS POWER OVER NATURE, DEMONS, AND ILLNESS—EVEN DEATH ITSELF.

In biblical times, miracles were understood to be signs of God's presence. Asking whether or not the miraculous actually took place, if it really happened, was not the point. One asked, instead, what the event meant. What did God mean by it?

The Gospels offer many examples of Jesus's wonder-working, and they are included to show clearly that Jesus was truly the long-awaited Messiah. John lists seven specific miracles, but only the feeding of the crowd of five thousand and the Resurrection appear in all four gospels. Yet, by the time Jesus is resurrected from the dead and ascends into heaven, His divine origin is meant to be undoubted.

> Jesus said unto her, I am the resurrection, and the life: he that believeth in me, though he were dead, yet shall he live.
>
> JOHN 11:25

During His lifetime, Jesus amassed His huge following—crowds sometimes numbering in the tens of thousands—because of His reputation as a healer. After preaching in a town's synagogue, Matthew writes, Jesus routinely walks through the area, healing the sick in the vicinity. His followers know, of course, that life on earth is temporal and ultimately comes to an end, but theologians believe that these physical healings are symbols of spiritual

The Miracle of the Loaves and Fishes

healing—the real reason for His mission. Jesus performs them with a spirit of compassion and love for all humanity. On many occasions, including the raisings from the dead, He even credits the individual's faith for the realization of the miracle.

According to John, Jesus reluctantly performs His first miracle at the Wedding in Cana at the behest of Mary, His mother. The wine has run out, and fearing embarrassment for the bride and groom, Mary beseeches Jesus for help. Saying it is "not my time," Christ grudgingly transforms the water in the jugs into wine.

In another miracle, Jesus earns the loyalty of His first five apostles by sending them out to fish again after a futile night's work. When they are shocked at the abundance filling their nets, Jesus tells them, "From now on, you will be fishers of people."

After feeding the five thousand, Jesus proves His power over nature by walking on water to His waiting disciples. In the Gospel According to Saint Matthew, Peter attempts to meet Him and steps onto the water, too. At first He walks, but suddenly doubt hits Him, and he sinks. Jesus, catching him, mocks him for his lack of faith—the importance of faith being the point of the story.

Jesus Walks on Water

Christ Healing the Blind

Entry into Jerusalem

CHRISTIANS COMMEMORATE JESUS'S TRIUMPHANT ENTRY INTO JERUSALEM ON PALM SUNDAY, THE SUNDAY BEFORE EASTER. FULLY AWARE OF HIS FATE, JESUS PREPARED HIS DISCIPLES AND FACED THE WRATH OF THE PHARISEES.

All four of the Gospels relate how, at the height of His ministry and popularity, Jesus began His final week as an earthly man.

Joining the throngs of pilgrims on their way to Jerusalem to celebrate the feast of Passover, Jesus reminds His disciples that He is to be arrested, tried, and killed there; three days later He will come back to life.

Jesus orders His disciples to find a donkey to ride into Jerusalem. Though the symbolism is lost on His disciples, the authorities and religious recognize Jesus's entrance on a donkey as the fulfillment of Zechariah's messianic prophecy. (In the biblical Middle East, the donkey is a royal animal symbolizing peace. A king at war would ride a horse.)

Wildly cheering crowds greet Jesus and cover His path with their cloaks, waving palm fronds in His honor and calling out psalms associated with the coming of the Messiah.

Outside of Jerusalem, Jesus asks for a donkey to ride upon

Entry into Jerusalem

The Pharisees and Sadducees, worried about losing their religious authority, are outraged.

Visiting the temple the next and temple elders continually challenge His knowledge and interpretations of the Law, which Jesus defends with great disciples that although they are admired now, many of the people will soon hate them. Jesus tells them of the coming

> Rejoice greatly, O daughter of Zion; shout, O daughter of Jerusalem: behold, thy King cometh unto thee: he is just, and having salvation; lowly, and riding upon an ass, and upon a colt the foal of an ass.
>
> ZECHARIAH 9:9

day, Jesus angrily throws out the money changers and dealers in sacrificial animals, making it clear that the temple is a house of prayer, not a place of business. Jesus's preaching attracts vast crowds over the next several days. The priests confidence. He enrages them with His parables and with His answers on paying taxes, rising from the dead, and obeying the commandments, advising the people not to follow the poor example set by the priests.

In private, He warns His destruction of the temple and the coming of the Son of Man, which will bring salvation. The Pharisees, seeking to avoid a riot yet wishing to eliminate their enemy, plot against Jesus, bribing Judas Iscariot to betray Him.

Christ Driving the Merchants from the Temple

The Last Supper

THE FINAL MEAL JESUS AND HIS DISCIPLES
SHARED—PRIOR TO HIS BETRAYAL, ARREST, TRIAL,
AND EXECUTION—IS CALLED THE LAST SUPPER,
ALSO KNOWN AS THE LORD'S SUPPER.

The Synoptic Gospels place the time of the Last Supper on the first night of Passover. John, however, places it on the night before, the night Passover lambs are slaughtered. (John frequently refers to Jesus as the lamb of God, associating him with the animal sacrifices Jews perform in the temple.)

In John's depiction, Jesus washes the feet of His disciples during the dinner. When Peter strenuously objects, Jesus tells him that in order to lead, one must be humble, acting as a servant to one's followers.

In the other three Gospels, Jesus meets His disciples in an upstairs room for a Passover

Christ Washing the Feet of the Apostles

> Jesus saith unto them, Come and dine. And none of the disciples durst ask him, Who art thou? knowing that it was the Lord.
>
> JOHN 21:12

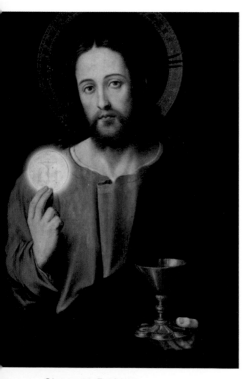

Christ with Eucharist

meal. He tells them how much He has looked forward to being with them before His suffering begins. Ceremoniously breaking the unleavened bread, He hands some to each one, saying, "This is my body which is given for you. This do in remembrance of me."

Passing a chalice of wine, He says, "This cup is the new testament in my blood, which is shed for you." He tells the disciples that one of them at the table will betray Him. "Which of us?" each asks in turn. Peter insists that he is ready to die for Jesus, but Jesus tells him, sadly, that before the cock crows

Jesus and the Twelve Apostles at the Last Supper

Then Peter, turning about, seeth the disciple whom Jesus loved following;
which also leaned on his breast at supper, and said, Lord,
which is he that betrayeth thee?

JOHN 21:20

that morning he will three times deny even knowing Him.

According to John, Jesus then delivers a long farewell discourse to His followers that includes the words, "I am the way, the truth, and the life: No one cometh to the Father, but by me." He also informs the disciples that He is asking God to send down the Holy Spirit to help each of them continue his mission. After predicting that their coming sadness will turn to joy, Jesus says that they will soon be sent out in the world. He prays to God for them.

A critical element in Christian worship services, the Sacrament of Holy Eucharist, or the offering of Jesus's body and blood, is a powerful reminder to his followers of the ultimate sacrifice Jesus made for humankind.

The Betrayal and Arrest of Jesus

IN THE GOSPELS, THE EVENTS LEADING TO THE DEATH OF JESUS ARE FILLED WITH HIGH DRAMA, BUT NONE SO POWERFUL AS THE BETRAYAL OF ONE OF HIS CLOSEST FOLLOWERS, JUDAS ISCARIOT.

Matthew recounts the beginning of Christ's betrayal when Jesus and His disciples retire to the Garden of Gethsemane, on the Mount of Olives, after the Passover meal.

Peter, John, and James follow Jesus to a quiet corner, where He sorrowfully asks them to watch over Him as He prays.

Deep in prayer, Jesus begs God to relieve Him of the suffering He is about to face, only to discover that His disciples, meanwhile, have all fallen asleep. Upset that they are unable to stay awake for even an hour, Jesus urges them to pray to avoid temptation, saying, "The spirit is willing but the flesh is weak." Once more Jesus goes away to pray, saying to God, "Your will be done." When He returns to His disciples, they have again fallen asleep. He wakes them, saying His hour has come.

Judas Iscariot arrives with a crowd of soldiers and an armed mob sent by the temple priests. "Who are you seeking?" Jesus asks the mob, identifying Himself.

According to the Synoptic Gospels, Judas kisses Jesus as a prearranged sign, saying, "Peace be with you, Teacher."

> But Jesus said unto him, Judas, betrayest thou the Son of man with a kiss?
>
> LUKE 22:48

Again Jesus declares His identity, and, as He is tied up, He tells the mob to leave His disciples alone. One of them

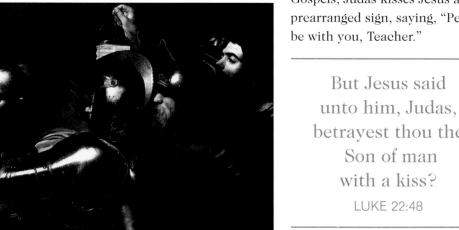

Taking of Christ in the Garden

Jesus prays in Gethsemane

(Peter, according to John) raises his sword, cutting off the ear of Malchus, the high priest's slave. Admonishing him with the words, "For all they that take the sword shall perish with the sword," Jesus heals Malchus's ear. He demands to know why the soldiers are arresting Him in the dead of night—couldn't they have approached Him while He was preaching in the synagogue? When they drag Jesus away for a secret trial, most of His disciples run away, but Peter surreptitiously follows Him.

The Synoptic Gospels never say why Judas Iscariot betrays Jesus. Luke says Satan possesses him. John says that Judas carries the bag of money for the group and alludes to his pilfering some of it for personal use. According to Matthew, Judas is so agonized by his decision that he returns the thirty pieces of silver and hangs himself, whereupon the priests use the money to buy a potter's field in which to bury the indigent dead.

The Crucifixion

THE FUNDAMENTAL SYMBOL OF CHRISTIANITY, CRUCIFIXION DEALT A CRUEL DEATH TO THE CONDEMNED, BUT IT WAS A METHOD OF EXECUTION WIDELY USED IN THE ANCIENT WORLD.

All four Gospels include the death of Jesus by crucifixion—a form of execution often meted out to slaves, rebels, criminals, and foreigners. It was a merciless death, and one feared by all, but it was particularly abhorrent to Jews because of a warning in Deuteronomy: "His body shall not remain all night upon the tree, but thou shalt in any wise bury him that day; (for he that is hanged is accursed of God)" (21:23).

Christians believe Christ's death is foretold in Isaiah's description of the suffering servant, as well as in parts of Psalm 22, and that Jesus, in order to extend God's covenant to all, has no choice but to fulfill

Christ Wearing the Crown of Thorns, Supported by Angels

the prophecy. As an example, Christian theologians cite Jesus's refusal to help Himself after the court condemns Him to death, even though Pilate is clearly willing to reconsider His fate. All four gospels describe Pontius Pilate handing Jesus over to soldiers who mockingly dress Him in a purple robe and a crown of thorns, hitting Him and spitting on Him. They force Him to carry His cross through Jerusalem (His path is known today as the Via Dolorosa, or Way of Sorrows) to the Hill of Golgotha (or Hill of Skulls). En route, the soldiers compel a man named Simon of Cyrene to help Jesus.

The mob crucifies two thieves alongside Jesus. Pilate places a

Christ Leaving the Court

Jesus crucified with two thieves

sign on Jesus's cross, which reads "Jesus of Nazareth, the King of the Jews." The soldiers roll dice for His clothing as Jesus is dying. People in the crowd insult Him, saying, "If thou be the son of God, come down from the cross."

According to Luke, one of the crucified thieves joins in the taunts; the other, who says Jesus is innocent and does not deserve His fate, corrects him. Jesus, promising they will be in paradise together that afternoon, cries out, "My God, why hast thou forsaken me?" When He is thirsty, He is offered vinegar on a sponge.

When Christ dies, earthquakes rumble and the sky goes dark between 12:00 and 3:00 in the afternoon, according to the Synoptic Gospels. In Matthew, the dead rise, and the curtain hanging in the temple, which separates the place where God dwells from His sinning people, is symbolically rent in two. After Christ's death, similarly, there is no separation between God and humanity: Jesus has atoned for all sin.

> Jesus, when he had cried again with a loud voice, yielded up the ghost. And, behold, the veil of the temple was rent in twain from the top to the bottom; and the earth did quake, and the rocks rent.
>
> MATTHEW 27:50–51

The Resurrection

EASTER SUNDAY, THE MOST IMPORTANT CHRISTIAN FEAST DAY, CELEBRATES CHRIST'S RESURRECTION FROM THE DEAD. A PHYSICAL MANIFESTATION OF HUMANITY'S PROMISED SALVATION, THE RESURRECTION IS THE FOUNDATION ON WHICH THE CHRISTIAN FAITH RESTS.

Jesus's humiliating death had disillusioned His followers, especially after they had that learned He has been buried like any other man. By rising from the dead, however, Jesus would fulfill Old Testament predictions of the appearance of a savior, thus reigniting their faith. Holding out the prospect of salvation to all people, Jesus creates a new covenant between God and all humanity.

According to the Gospels, Pilate had been surprised at the speed with which Jesus died; unlike the two thieves, the executioners hadn't needed to break His legs in order to hasten the process.

Once Jesus is dead, Joseph of Arimethea, a secret disciple of Jesus and a member of the counsel, takes Jesus's body down from the cross, offering to place it in an empty tomb he owns. Joseph wraps Jesus's body in linen and places it in the tomb, sealing the entrance with a heavy stone.

Accounts of the Resurrection differ slightly in each Gospel, but all agree that it is Mary Magdalene, either alone or with two other women, who first sees the risen Jesus. According to Mark and Luke, the boulder has inexplicably moved when the women come to anoint the body. Matthew says an earthquake moves the stone when the women arrive, terrifying the guards. An angel in white informs the women that Christ has risen, beseeching them to tell the other disciples. In

Noli Me Tangere ("Touch Me Not")

Mark, the frightened women run away; in Luke and Matthew, it is the risen Jesus who asks them to inform the others.

John's account portrays Mary Magdalene, who believes Jesus's body has been stolen, alone and crying at the empty tomb. A man she imagines is the gardener asks her what is wrong. Looking up, she sees it is Jesus. He warns her not to touch Him—He has not yet gone to his father. Still a flesh-and-blood man, Jesus has the power to vanish and reappear, which He does several times while visiting the disciples He is now preparing to go out into the world to spread His word.

Lamentation (The Mourning of Christ)

Ascension of Jesus

Acts of the Apostles

Written by Luke, the Acts of the Apostles, the fifth book of the New Testament, can be regarded as a continuation of his Gospel. If the Old Testament deals with humanity's relationship to God, and the gospels are concerned with the works of Jesus—God manifested as man—then Acts of the Apostles demonstrates the effects of the Holy Spirit on God's people once they have attained spiritual knowledge.

Acts opens with the ascension of Jesus into Heaven and proceeds to the Pentecost, where Jesus's disciples, imbued with the Holy Spirit, revel in their newfound ability to spread Christ's message. We meet Stephen, the first martyr for his faith, and Saul, one of Christ's tormentors who, changing his name to Paul, becomes his greatest defender. Peter converts the first Gentiles, and Acts explains Christianity as an evolved form of Judaism that welcomes everyone.

Supplying an early history of the Christian faith when it is still considered a Judaic sect, Acts of the Apostles also offers the first written insight into the formulation of early Christian beliefs, the roots of a tradition that subsequently flowers into a huge worldwide movement.

Pentecost celebrates the coming of the Holy Spirit to the Apostles

Pentecost

THE PENTECOST, COMMEMORATED TODAY WITH THE WEARING OF RED, MARKS THE FIFTIETH DAY AFTER THE RESURRECTION OF CHRIST, WHEN HIS FOLLOWERS ACCEPTED THE HOLY SPIRIT THAT CAME TO THEM THROUGH FLAMES.

Israelites first used the term *Pentecost*, a Greek and Latin word meaning "fiftieth day," to honor God's gift of the Ten Commandments to Moses at Mount Sinai, which occurred fifty days after the Exodus. This festival, which occurs fifty days after "first fruits," eventually became a harvest celebration known as the Sukkot.

For Christians, Pentecost is the fifty days between the Resurrection of Jesus on Easter Sunday and the coming of the Holy Spirit ten days after his ascension into Heaven.

Acts describes how the disciples, waiting in Jerusalem for the gift Christ has promised them, fast and pray for nine days. His mother, Mary, and other women are present. On the tenth day, the disciples and believers gather in the upper room where they had held the Last Supper. Suddenly, a noise from the sky sounding like a windstorm fills the house, and what appear to be tongues of fire spread out to touch each person

> And when the day of Pentecost was fully come, they were all with one accord in one place.
>
> ACTS 2:1

present. Filled with the Holy Spirit, all discover that they now possess the ability to speak in many different languages.

Hearing the noise, a large crowd gathers. Among them are Jews from many different countries who are living in Jerusalem. All are shocked to discover this group of Galileans can speak their native tongues. Peter quotes the prophet Joel, who speaks of God's promise to pour out His spirit on everyone.

He recounts the story of Jesus's life, proclaiming Him to

Saint Paul preaching in Athens

Pentecost is the coming of the Holy Spirit fifty days after Easter

be the true Messiah who King David had predicted would rise from the dead. If the people turn away from sin and are baptized in Christ's name, Peter says, their sins will be forgiven; they, too, will receive the Holy Spirit. Three thousand people are baptized that day.

The disciples turn into teachers, fonts of divine wisdom. Imbued with the Holy Spirit, they are fearless and no longer dread persecution, pain, or death. Instead, they avidly preach Jesus's way to anyone who will listen. As described in Acts, people now followed the Gospel in Jerusalem, Judea, Samaria, Syria, Asia Minor, Europe, and Rome, heart of the empire.

Pentecost Sunday, a major feast in the Christian religion, is traditionally celebrated by wearing red garments, in honor of the tongues of flame bearing the gift of the Holy Spirit.

THE CHURCH AT ANTIOCH

In Antioch, the capital of Syria under Roman rule, Christianity flourishes and an organized leadership evolves. The Council of Jerusalem attempts to bridge the traditions of Jewish and Gentile converts with the expectations of the new religion.

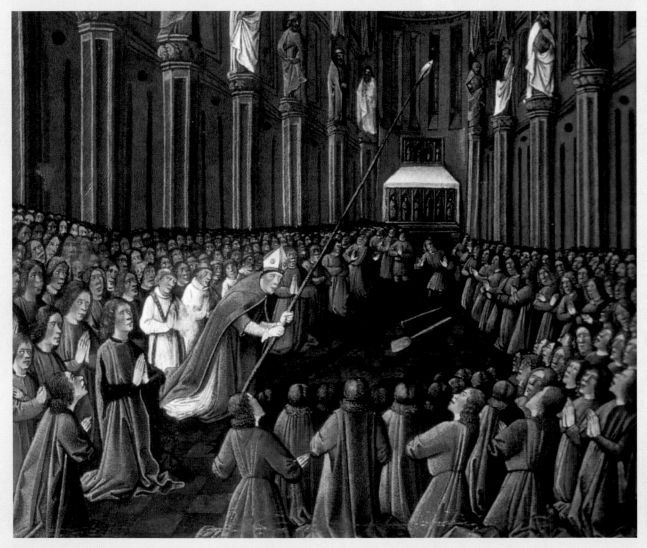

The Holy Lance at Antioch

IF JERUSALEM IS CONSIDERED the birthplace of Christianity, Antioch becomes its center.

At the dawn of Christianity, Antioch was the administrative capital of the Roman province of Syria and the third-largest city in the empire after Rome and Alexandria. It was a Hellenistic metropolis at the mouth of the Orontes River, the intersection of three trade routes, and filled with worldly distractions. Its racially mixed population of nearly 500,000 was predominantly Gentile but also included a large Jewish community. Though paganism still thrived there, the city would soon become the center of Christianity. Antioch was, in fact, where Christ's followers were first called "Christians."

Paul and Barnabas at Lystra

Stephen, the first Christian martyr, preached in Jerusalem's Hellenist synagogues. HIs words outraged his listeners, and, in 35 CE, he was stoned to death. His death led to the widespread persecution of Nazarenes in Jerusalem and resulted in a flood of Christians seeking refuge in Samaria and Syria, including the city of Antioch.

Apostles Barnabas and Paul arrived in Antioch in 38 CE, winning many converts. Largely through the inspired missionary work of Paul, Christianity grows from a small Jewish sect into a new religion whose converts are principally Gentiles. With Barnabas, Paul established a strong Christian community at Antioch. From there, disciples would depart for missionary journeys through the Roman Empire. Paul himself made three missionary trips from Antioch, and Peter led its church for many years after he arrived there in 44 CE.

In his Epistle to the Galatians, Paul writes about his great disagreement with Christ's Jewish followers in Jerusalem. It is Paul's conviction that circumcision should not be required for Gentiles. Cynical skeptics in Jerusalem, however, feel Paul's great success with

Saint Barnabas treating the Sick

conversion arises from the fact that many displaced Jews living abroad simply find it too difficult to observe Mosaic law.

In 50 CE, as described in Acts, the leaders of the new church meet in Jerusalem to debate these issues in what becomes known as the Council of Jerusalem. James, the "Pillar of the Church" who advocates enforcing the laws of the Torah, nevertheless agrees with Peter's argument: Jews and Gentiles should be allowed to follow the customs of their respective traditions. His letter to the Gentiles, known as the Apostolic Decree, requests only that they eat no food offered to idols, eat no blood, and refrain from sexual immorality.

The
Epistles

An *epistle,* from the Greek word for "letter," is a form of formal public communication often used in the early Christian era to address groups or specific individuals. This literary style, which can be traced back to Egypt in the fourth century BCE, eventually became popular in Greece. Written in a strict Greek format, the epistles in the New Testament open with a greeting from the writer naming the letter's intended recipient; the scribe taking dictation and the delivering messenger are often named at the end.

Of the 21 epistles included in the New Testament, biblical scholars attribute 13 of them to the Apostle Paul. Written to church groups, communities, and individuals, the letters deal with settling disputes, maintaining unity, correcting theological teachings, and warning against false teachers. They are expected to be widely circulated, and they offer Paul an invaluable method of keeping in touch with the many churches he founds throughout Asia Minor.

The Apostle Paul

The Holy Spirit

A CONCEPT THAT HAS ALLOWED MANY INTERPRETATIONS,
THE HOLY SPIRIT WAS, FOR PAUL, THE SPIRIT OF GOD
MADE PRESENT AMONG THE PEOPLE.

In the Old Testament, the Holy Spirit assists in creation, inspires Moses and Joshua, gives Samson physical strength, is bestowed upon and taken away from Saul, gives David the plans for the temple, and motivates the prophets. While Jews believe it to be an expression of God's spirit, Christians see the Holy Spirit as an entity separate from God, believing that the father, Son, and Holy Spirit are three entities in the one triune deity.

In Western Christianity, although the son is eternally begotten from the father, the Holy Spirit proceeds from the father and the son.

Orthodox Christians, who dispute this, maintain that the Holy Spirit proceeds solely from the father.

In the Synoptic Gospels, as John baptizes Christ, the Holy Spirit, in the form of a white dove, descends upon Jesus, and, shortly thereafter, Jesus begins His mission. After the Resurrection, Jesus attempts

> For what man knoweth the things of a man, save the spirit of man which is in him? even so the things of God knoweth no man, but the Spirit of God.
> 1 CORINTHIANS 2:11

to prepare His disciples for the coming presence of the Holy Spirit, which He refers to as the "comforter" and the "spirit of truth," the spirit that will lead them to the truth of God. Upon His ascension into Heaven, Jesus sends the Holy Spirit down to His disciples, who are filled with wisdom and understanding. And in the

The Holy Spirit as a Dove

The Trinity is God, Jesus, and the Holy Spirit

Epistles, Paul continuously stresses the importance of the Holy Spirit in uniting believers, granting graces, and bringing humans closer to God. In his First Epistle to the Corinthians (12:13), Paul states, "For by one Spirit are we all baptized into one body, whether *we be* Jews or Gentiles, whether *we be* bond or free; and have been all made to drink into one Spirit."

The New Testament calls upon Christians to welcome the Holy Spirit in order to receive the spiritual gifts of wisdom, understanding, counsel, fortitude, knowledge, piety, and fear of the Lord. Most important, when we are baptized, the Holy Spirit dwells within us, and we become temples of God.

The Baptism of Jesus

Paul's Message

CHRISTIANITY WOULD HAVE VERY LIKELY REMAINED A MINOR JEWISH SECT WERE IT NOT FOR PAUL. HIS WRITINGS, WHICH CHRISTIANS NOW CONSIDER DIVINELY INSPIRED, MAKE UP 13 OF THE 27 BOOKS OF THE NEW TESTAMENT.

In his role as Apostle to the Gentiles, Paul was a tireless proselytizer whose zeal won him thousands of Christian converts throughout the Mediterranean basin.

As an ardent Pharisee from the tribe of Benjamin, Saul (his given name), born in Tarsus in southeast Turkey, zealously observed the Law of Moses. His family also enjoyed

Roman citizenship, and he was completely comfortable with the Greek language and culture.

Hoping to become a rabbi, Saul studied in Jerusalem under Gamaliel, the famous Sanhedrin

Saint Paul and his Disciples

Saint Paul writing his Epistles

leader and scholar. This was a time when Jews regarded it as extremely important that the surrounding pagan societies respect Jewish religious practices. Therefore, when a small cult began extolling the crucified Jesus as the Messiah, Saul took it an insult to the faith—clearly God would never mark the Jewish savior for a criminal's death.

His outrage initially made Saul one of the apostles' fiercest antagonists and persecutors. Yet, after his shocking conversion on the road to Damascus, Saul insisted that his knowledge of the Gospel came directly from the risen Christ, who appeared to him there. As a result—because he saw Jesus and learned from Him directly—Saul (now Paul) always considered himself to be an apostle.

As an apostle, he brought the same level of zealous intensity to his new life as a Christian missionary that he had exhibited as a ruthless persecutor of Christians. He insisted that the Resurrection of Jesus obviates the need to observe Jewish law and that this new way of life should be as open to Gentiles as it was to Jews. In his many epistles, Paul attempts to encourage the faithful, warn them against false teachings, and answer the questions they send him.

Critics often fault Paul for straying from Jesus's original message. His letters insisting that women refrain from church leadership stress the patriarchal nature of much of Christianity, even today. Similarly, Paul's is the only New Testament writing to condemn homosexuality.

HOUSE CHURCHES

After the Pentecost, early believers would listen to the apostles at the temple gates, but as Christians began to be persecuted and driven from the temples, they started to meet in private houses.

THE EARLY CHURCH did not depend on dedicated buildings to thrive and form a community of worshipers. Christians would meet their fellow believers in their homes, gathering together to share meals, sing hymns, read scripture, discuss their individual revelations, and pray. The epistles of the New Testament are delivered to these houses, where the people read them to each other, copying them over before sending them on to other house churches.

House churches are first mentioned in Acts 1:13, when the apostles and their followers meet in Jerusalem to pray in an "upper room" following Jesus's ascension. Typically, several church members would meet in the most affluent member's house, which was usually the largest; the members would usually confer a leadership role on the homeowner. Meetings in house churches would take place around the banquet or

The Holy Spirit comes to the Apostles in a house where they are praying

dining-room table, with each person donating a gift for the "fellowship meal"—some food, a song or prayer, perhaps a prophecy. Early Christians also crossed social and, eventually, religious barriers by permitting Jews and Gentiles to gather together under one roof.

Not limited to the conventional family, the household, which customarily took on the religion of the household's head, could also include slaves, freed persons, tenants, artisans, and other relatives. Though the culture was predominantly patriarchal, women did, in reality, head many households. In fact, early Christianity seems to attract wealthy, independent women, who were often widows. And though life in the center of the

---

For where two or three are gathered together in my name, there am I in the midst of them.

MATTHEW 18:20

---

empire was definitely more restrictive, it was not uncommon for these women to travel freely and run businesses in outlying Roman colonies.

As new house churches formed, the strongest leader in a district would take on the supervision and management of multiple churches. One of Paul's overriding concerns was the possibility that these multichurch congregations might break off into cliques, thus diminishing chances for unity among the flock as a whole.

The Holy Spirit makes the Apostles fearless

WOMEN IN THE EARLY CHURCH

Although all of the Twelve Apostles were men, the Gospels make it clear that women were deeply involved in Christ's ministry from its earliest days in Galilee to its worldwide continuance after His death.

ALWAYS KIND TO WOMEN, Jesus treated them with grace, dignity, and compassion, far from the social norm of his time. Thus, it is no surprise to discover that women were, along with the other marginalized people who make up the crowds following him, some of his most ardent supporters, serving him in every capacity available

> There is neither Jew nor Greek, there is neither bond nor free, there is neither male nor female: for ye are all one in Christ Jesus.
>
> GALATIANS 3:28

to them. Mary Magdalene, for example, accompanied Him throughout His ministry and supported Him with her own money. She was also the first to witness Jesus after His Resurrection, and although a woman's testimony has little value in the society of His time, it is she whom Jesus instructed to inform the others.

As a Jewish sect, early Christianity was rooted in the customs of a patriarchal society. Women never served as temple priests. Indeed, although they worked side by side with the apostles and were frequently cited in Paul's Epistles, the major responsibilities of the church were discharged almost entirely

by men. Wealthy women did, however, support the burgeoning faith, both spiritually and financially, funding apostolic missions, donating to the poor, and often supplying the homes in which the earliest Christian meetings took place.

Women such as Lydia, Nympha, Apphia, and Prisca often found themselves in leadership roles according to the Acts of the Apostles and Paul's Epistles. Female prophets and deacons were common, and a close reading of the New Testament reveals their substantial power.

In 1 Timothy 2:11, Paul, though he frequently sends regards, praise, and thanks to

Saint Prisca

individual women, admonishes them against speaking in church or daring to teach men, instead counseling subservience. (Historians believe that Paul did not want to inflame the authorities by challenging traditional gender roles.)

In Rome, Christianity offered an exciting option to young upper-class women, who were typically contracted into marriage at an early age. Refusing matrimony for the sake of faith granted them an unimaginable degree of autonomy, although many of these women would suffer a martyr's death for their refusal to abide the wishes of their parents.

Agony in the Garden, with Saints Martha and Mary

THE EPISTLES OF PAUL THE APOSTLE TO THE

COLOSSIANS & PHILEMON

THE LETTERS THAT PAUL WROTE TO THE EARLY CHURCH IN COLOSSAE AND TO PHILEMON ARE CONNECTED BY THE CARRIER, ONESIMUS, WHO WAS SLAVE TO PHILEMON AND A CHRISTIAN CONVERT.

Saint Onesimus

The Epistle to the Colossians is directed to a church Paul does not found, in Colossae, a town near Ephesus. While imprisoned in Rome, one of the church's founders, who is troubled by the inclusion in its Christian worship of neighboring religious practices, visits Paul. Paul's letter asserts Jesus's primary role in Christianity and clarifies the nature of Jesus as God.

The Christians of Colossae assumed that Jesus was a spirit, not a man; they believed, therefore, that they should try to live in the spirit, and that the material world was evil. To buttress these beliefs, the ascetic Colossians incorporated painful fasting and self-denial into their worship. They also believed in a hierarchy of spiritual beings—such as angels—whom believers would need to contact as spiritual intermediaries. Additionally, the Colossae Christians also adopted the rite of circumcision and the observance of various moon festivals.

In his letter, Paul stays clearly focused on Jesus. It is Jesus, he says, who frees us from all prior religious laws, making it possible to live a truly spiritual life. As in his Epistle to the Ephesians, Paul describes how Jesus's followers may best treat one another and those around them, by setting examples for the nonbelievers in their midst. He insists that church members are to

---

Set your affection on things above, not on things on the earth. For ye are dead, and your life is hid with Christ in God. When Christ, who is our life, shall appear, then shall ye also appear with him in glory.

COLOSSIANS 3: 2–4

---

follow Jesus—not any man-made rituals. Paul also implores the congregation to circulate his letter to church communities in neighboring towns. This, he hopes, will serve to correct the many misconceptions under which these early Christians are laboring.

Paul mentions a friend named Onesimus, who would carry the letter back to the Colossians for him. A runaway slave who ended up in Rome, a thousand miles away from his home in Colossae, Onesimus visited Paul frequently after his conversion to Christianity. Onesimus will also

Circumcision of Christ

deliver a second missive, the Epistle to Philemon, a wealthy church leader in Colossae, which is essentially a request to Philemon to release his slave from service. When he sends him back to his master, Paul writes a flattering letter to Philemon, reminding him that it is Paul who converts Philemon, and because Onesimus is also a Christian, he should be treated more as a brother than as a servant.

THE EPISTLE OF
JAMES

JAMES IS THE FIRST OF THE EPISTLES NOW CATEGORIZED AS THE "GENERAL" OR "CATHOLIC" EPISTLES. THESE LETTERS, RATHER THEN BEING ADDRESSED TO A PARTICULAR CHURCH OR PERSON, ARE AIMED AT CHRISTIANS IN GENERAL.

The twentieth book of the New Testament begins with the salutation, "James, a slave of God and of the Lord, Jesus Christ." Though there are two apostles named James, some believe that this letter is written

Saint James the Lesser

by James the Just, also known as Jesus's brother, who heads the church in Jerusalem. James the Lesser, or younger, apostle was beheaded in 44 CE, and James the Just was martyred by stoning in 66 CE, thus making this document one of the oldest in the New Testament.

The Epistle of James is addressed to Jewish Christians, who have been scattered all over the world. Occasionally characterized as Wisdom Literature, the book, more a series of statements on a wide range of ethical issues, is closer in tone to the Book of Proverbs than a standard letter supporting a theme.

James presents trials and tribulations as tests from God; believers gain strength and endurance by passing them. James also warns against making snap judgments about fellow worshipers. All who enter church are equal in the eyes of God—the poor as well as the very wealthy. In order to truly live as Christians, one must watch every action—gossip is a particular danger. It is foolish to become obsessed with worldly matters; this life is fleeting and one must work to please God, not the world. Since one never knows what tomorrow

*The Apparition of the
Virgin to Saint James
the Greater*

brings, boasting and forcing the will is futile. One should, instead, plan with the thought, "I will do this if it pleases the Lord." Many of the statements James makes can be linked to Jesus's Sermon on the Mount, particularly His admonishments against excessive wealth.

The centerpiece of James's letter is the insistence that faith requires action. "Even so faith, if it hath not works, is dead, being alone" (James 2:17). This conviction—that simple belief is not enough to put one in God's good grace—underlies a basic philosophical disagreement among Christians today: Catholics stress that faith must include good works; Protestants, citing Paul, believe faith in Christ saves us.

James ends his letter advising everyone to pray—not just for themselves, but for one another. Doing so strengthens the entire community.

PERSECUTION AND MARTYRDOM

Christians of the early church did not have an easy road, and any convert might face persecution. Although many early Christians worshiped undisturbed, many died during the reigns of certain Roman emperors, such as Decius, Diocletian, and Nero.

OFTEN EXECUTED in very gruesome ways, martyrs (those killed for proselytizing Christianity) are also referred to as "blood witnesses" for Christ. Some consider martyrdom, a "baptism in blood," a form of purification.

The first recorded Christian martyr is Stephen (Acts 6:8–8:3), stoned to death around 35 CE. Jewish leaders, hoping to stomp out this small, heretical sect, advocate persecution of the early Christians, which initially takes the form of financial discrimination and social shunning.

In the Apostolic Age of the first century, 11 of the 12 original apostles were martyred after frequent incarcerations, beatings, and house arrests. James the Lesser, James the Greater, and Matthias were martyred by the Jews of Jerusalem, and Peter and Paul were executed in Rome.

The other martyred apostles died for their evangelical work

> And fear not them which kill the body, but are not able to kill the soul.
>
> MATTHEW 10:28

in various locations around the world. The only one to escape martyrdom was John, who survived being boiled in oil. He is said to have lived a long life in exile.

Christian Martyrs in the Colosseum

In the first three centuries after the birth of Christ, Roman authorities harass Christians for refusing to make worship offerings to Roman gods or to consider emperors divine. Nero, who began the persecution by blaming Christians for the fire that destroyed much of Rome, made the public spectacle of torturing Christians in arenas a part of Greco-Roman civic life.

Early Christians understood the necessity of suffering: it was their part to play in accomplishing God's purpose, a chance, in a hostile and often violent world, to bring Jesus's

Young Christian Martyr

message to others. Suffering in His name was considered an honor—one that would bring an eternal reward after death. Deaths in the name of

Christianity were rampant in the Age of Martyrdom (the second through fourth centuries CE), particularly under Diocletian.

Inspirational tales of the courage of these first Christian saints, many of them young women who are fearless in the face of imperial power, did much to facilitate the spread of Christianity through the Roman Empire. The persecution ended in 313 CE with Constantine's legalization of Christianity. Later in the fourth century, under Theodosius, Christianity became the official religion of the empire.

The Christian Martyrs' Last Prayer

THE EPISTLE OF
JUDE

THE EPISTLE OF JUDE IS A SHORT LETTER WHOSE WRITER
REFERS TO HIMSELF AS THE "BROTHER OF JAMES"
AND THE "SERVANT OF JESUS CHRIST."

Saint Jude Thaddeus speaks of salvation

The Epistle of Jude is the twenty-sixth and penultimate book of the New Testament. Consisting of only 25 stanzas, with a sterner, more severe tone than most of the New Testament books, it was written as an encyclical to be read in many churches. Jude begins by saying that he means the subject of his letter to be salvation; instead, however, he is moved to discuss the fact that the greatest threats to Christianity are the many false teachings that are now welling up from inside the church itself. In a tone very similar to Peter's in his second letter, Jude's letter warns against the false teachers, then surfacing within many Christian groups, who have interpreted forgiveness of sin as a mandate to do whatever they like. They brag, carouse, defy authority, live immorally, use flattery, and cause division through the expression of their wanton desires.

Jude uses examples from the Old Testament and nonbiblical sources of Jewish apocrypha to remind readers how God punishes sin. He evokes the punishment endured by the faithless Israelis in the desert, as well as the fate of the fallen angels, chained in the darkness

Saint Jude warns against false teachings

of hell, awaiting the Final Judgment. He also cites the apocalyptic destruction of Sodom and Gomorrah and the evil of Cain, who murders his own brother. In a puzzling addition to this list, Jude tells of a battle between Michael the Archangel and Satan for the body of Moses. He beseeches church members to show these apostates mercy tempered with fear. Pray and try to save them, Jude says, but never listen to them, for they are bound to cause divisiveness.

Some versions of the Bible refer to him

Relief with Saints Philip, Jude, and Bartholomew

But ye, beloved, building up yourselves on your most holy faith, praying in the Holy Ghost, Keep yourselves in the love of God, looking for the mercy of our Lord Jesus Christ unto eternal life.

JUDE 1:20–21

Scholars disagree whether this Jude is one of the original Twelve Apostles—the letter seems to have been written in the mid-60s CE. The New Testament scarcely mentions the apostle known as Jude.

by his nickname, Thaddeus, so as not to confuse him with the traitor Judas Iscariot. Jude is known to have shared a mission with Simon the Zealot; both were martyred, in Beirut, in 65 CE.

APOCALYPSE

As were the earliest conceptions of Heaven and Hell,
the earliest notions of apocalypse, of catastrophic upheaval at the end the world,
extend back to the Persian religion of Zoroastrianism, in the third millennium BCE.

OLD TESTAMENT PROPHETS frequently alluded to a "Day of the Lord," which, they said, will catch the living unawares, bringing on a cataclysmic chain of violent events from which avoid God's judgment. Written in the second century BCE at a time of national despair, Daniel, using a complicated code full of numerical symbols and fantastical images, conveys a early Christians took up the mantle of apocalyptic prophecy. John, too, uses an elaborate code of imagery and symbols (many of today's Christian sects still consider them true predictors

> The sun shall be turned into darkness, and the moon into blood,
> before the great and the terrible day of the Lord come.
> And it shall come to pass, that whoever shall
> call on the name of the Lord shall be delivered.
>
> JOEL 2:31-32

no one will escape unscathed. The New Testament's last book, Revelation, details the famines, wars, earthquakes, and plagues to which earth will be subjected before humanity's final judgment.

The Old Testament book of Daniel is also considered apocalyptic literature (the Greek word *apokalypsis* means "something uncovered"), in that Daniel, unlike other prophetic books, does not counsel repentance in order to

powerful message: despite the present bleakness, God is far more powerful than any earthly king, including the pagan king who is attempting to exterminate Judaism. In a number of years, Daniel says, the natural order will be obliterated; when this occurs, their persecutors will feel the full weight of God's wrath—a most important point for believers.

With the Revelation of John, also written at a time when the faithful faced extermination,

of the coming apocalypse) to convey his vision of the downfall of an oppressive majority. Written at a time when many Christians were abandoning the faith, Revelation envisions a harrowing fate for those who displease God. The book also warrants that, while he may not have appeared in their lifetime, Jesus truly will return as the scriptures prophesied.

OPPOSITE PAGE:
The Four Horsemen of the Apocalypse

THE BOOK OF

REVELATION

THE CHRISTIAN BIBLE ENDS WITH REVELATION, A BOOK FILLED
WITH DREAMLIKE VISIONS OF THE APOCALYPTIC END-TIMES
THAT SYMBOLIZE THE FINAL VICTORY OF GOD.

The Book of Revelation ends the New Testament. Written at the end of the first century CE, it has traditionally been attributed to John the Apostle, the writer of the Gospel According to Saint John and the Epistles of John, although there is speculation that a different John may be the actual writer, because the author of Revelation makes no mention of his years as an original disciple.

Addressing seven churches along the coast of Turkey, John writes in code from the prison island of Patmos where he has been exiled for preaching Christianity, considered a crime against the empire

at the time of composition (likely the reign of Domitian, in 95 CE). Those who failed to renounce Jesus and adore the emperor as a god were severely punished and tortured, and even executed.

Drawing on Old Testament imagery from the Books of Daniel, I Esdras, and Ezekiel, John describes an apocalyptic future portending the end of the world and Christ's Second Coming. There are seven seals on a scroll, which are opened to unleash the first of many tribulations. Seven trumpeting angels each announce an impending disaster—hail and fire destroying a third of the earth's plant life; a mountain that

The Four Horsemen of the Apocalypse

crashes into the sea, killing off a third of ocean life; a falling star polluting fresh water; darkness covering the sun, moon, and stars; locusts swarming over the earth; a third of the earth's population dying from plague; and, finally, the seventh trumpet's blast signaling that the world is now God's kingdom. Further tribulation awaits the inhabitants of the world, including: seven plague-filled bowls of God's anger; the mark of the beast (666, considered by scholars code for Nero); the fall of Rome (code name: Babylon); and the

Final Judgment. Revelation ends with images of the true believers enjoying life in the shining city of the New Jerusalem, a model of perfection.

John stresses that the battle between good and evil is accelerating, warning his fellow Christians that their faith will be put to an even more severe test and reassuring them God will indeed intervene on their behalf. A great debate rages today between Christians who take Revelation to be an accurate prediction of the world's end and those who read it strictly symbolically.

The Beast with Ten Horns and the Beast with Lamb Horns

Heaven and Hell

NOTIONS OF HEAVEN AND HELL—PLACES FOR REWARD AND PUNISHMENT IN THE AFTERLIFE—EVOLVE THROUGHOUT THE BIBLE.

The Old Testament, which says very little about an afterlife or final judgment, concentrates instead on giving advice for living morally in the here and now. The Hebrew Bible refers to *sheol*, or the "grave," as an abode for the dead. All those who die, regardless of how they have lived, exist in sheol, described as a dark place cut off from the God who is living in the "heavens."

It is possible that, at the time of the Babylonian exile, Jews came into contact with practitioners of the Zoroastrian religion, who believed in the

The Blessed at the Gate to Heaven with Saint Peter

> "And many of them that sleep in the dust of the earth shall awake, some to everlasting life, and some to shame and everlasting contempt."
>
> DANIEL 12:2

The Ladder of Divine Ascent

concept of afterlife reward or punishment: those who have lived morally will be rewarded according to their degree of virtue; evildoers will be similarly punished. The Book of Daniel (12:1-3), written possibly as late as the second century BCE, offers the first biblical concepts of resurrection and final judgment, which are also Zoroastrian beliefs. Among Jews, although the Sadducees do not find enough biblical proof to believe in an afterlife, the Pharisees—whose Heaven consists not of an

Christ's Descent into Hell

ethereal sky-world but is, rather, a beautiful, paradisiacal garden on earth—do.

Followers of Baal and Moloch sacrificed their firstborn children in fires at Gehenna,

Paradise

also known as the Valley of the Son of Hinnom, outside the walls of Jerusalem, an area that eventually becomes a place for residents of Jerusalem to burn their rubbish. In the Old and New Testaments, Gehenna is a place where the wicked go to be burned away. Pharisees believed that the souls of those who have lived evil lives go to Gehenna for final destruction, while others receive a year of purification prior to entering Eden.

The origins of the Christian concepts of Heaven and Hell are found in the Book of Revelation. There are very few earthly rewards for early Christians; instead, believers who have accepted Jesus receive

assurances of eternal life in paradise after death. All those whose names are not found in the book of the saved are to be thrown into a lake of fire.

Christ Glorified in the Court of Heaven

clan of, 78
Epistles, 261—311
  of James, 294
  of John, 302, 308
  of Jude, 304
  of Paul the Apostle to Philemon, 285
  of Paul the Apostle to the Colossians and Philemon, 284
  of Paul the Apostle to the Corinthians, first, 264
  of Paul the Apostle to the Corinthians, second, 270—271
  of Paul the Apostle to the Ephesians, 278—279
  of Paul the Apostle to the Galatians, 272
  of Paul the Apostle to the Romans, 262—263
  of Paul the Apostle to the Thessalonians, 286
  of Paul the Apostle to Timothy and Titus, 290
  of Peter, 296, 300—301
  to the Hebrews, 292
Esau, 34—35, 169
Esdras, 176
Esdras, Book of, 308
Essenes, 190, 192
Esther, Book of, 10, 65, 171, 176, 188, 193
Ethiopia, 90
Euphrates River, 16, 98
Europe, 253
Eve, 20, 24—25, 26, 128
exile, 65, 68
Exodus, 214, 252
Exodus, Book of, 11, 19, 38—45, 46, 56, 59, 67, 72
Ezekiel, 55, 193
  Book of, 141, 308

visions of, 142—143
Ezra, Book of, 65, 166, 176

F

famine, 21, 37
Feast of the Nativity, 219
Feast of the Tabernacles, 118
Fertile Crescent, 16
Final Judgment, 228, 309
Flavius Josephus, 195
flood, 26
flute, 119
Forest of Lebanon, 92
Four Evangelists, 143, 197
frame drum, 118
fringes (on garments), 60

G

Gabriel, Archangel, 145, 208, 210, 214, 218
Gad (son of Jacob), 72
Galatia, 272
Galatians, 259
Galileans, 252
Galilee, 185, 200, 213, 230—231, 282
Galilee, Sea of, 185
Gamaliel, 274
Garden of Eden, 20, 24—25, 127, 128, 165
Gaspar, 213
Gath-hepher, 230
Gehenna, 311
Genesis, Book of, 11, 19, 20—37, 45, 46, 127, 128, 292
Gentiles, 183, 202, 247, 255, 257, 259, 263, 272, 273, 274, 279, 286, 297
Gentiles, Court of the, 191
Gibeah, 128
Gideon, 75, 76

Gilead, 77
Gnostic, 225
goat, 165
God, 19, 32—33, 40—41, 66—67, 94—95, 114, 115
  as creator, 19, 20—23
  commandments of, 125
  disgust of wickedness, 20
  forgiveness of, 74—75
  judgment of, 21, 63, 119
  king of all nations, 155
  lamb of, 207
  law of, 11, 129
  laws of, 19, 38—39, 40—41, 42—43, 45, 46, 56—57, 58, 62, 78, 169
  love for humankind, 56
  orders from, 70—71
  people of, 21, 65, 67, 89
  power of, 68, 117
  protection of, 79
  punishments of, 49, 53, 62, 83, 100—101
  relationship with, 113, 117, 127
  retribution of, 26, 80
  son of, 200, 211, 220
  spirit of, 29
  word of, 9, 62, 102
  wrath of, 42—43, 45, 49, 52, 100
golden calf, 39, 42—43
Goliath, 84
Gomer, 146, 147
Good Samaritan, 205
Gospel of Joy, 280
Gospels, 10, 13, 180, 197—245, 232, 247, 251, 253
Great Flood, 21, 26—27
Greece, 191, 257, 261, 263
Greek, 193, 194, 274, 296

peacock, 28
pelican, 28
penance, 268
Penance, 269
Pentateuch, 19—63, 40, 113
Pentateuch, the, 9
Pentecost, 149, 223, 247, 248,
    252—253, 254, 276, 300
persecution, 298—299
Persia, 168
Persians, 177
Peter the Apostle, 13, 29, 199, 202,
    207, 223, 231, 236, 238, 239,
    240, 241, 247, 249, 262, 273,
    296, 297, 298, 300, 301
  mission of, 254—255
pharaoh, 90
Pharisees, 63, 183, 190, 201, 202,
    226, 235, 248, 274, 310, 311
Philemon, 285
Philippi, 280, 286
Philip (son of Herod), 186
Philip the Apostle, 223
Philistia, 154
Philistines, 75, 77, 80, 82, 84, 85
Phoenicia, 154
pigeon, 28
Pistis Sophia, 225
plagues, 39
polygamy, 122
Pompey, General, 186
Pontius Pilate, 186, 205, 241, 242,
    244
pope, 223
Prefects, 186
priest, 47
Prince of Prophets, 135
Prisca, 282
Prodigal Son, 205
Promised Land, 21, 41, 49, 53, 57,
    68—69, 101
prophecy, 89, 99

Prophet of the Pentecost, 149
Prophets, 11, 19, 65, 76, 80, 82, 84,
    89, 94, 131—169, 135
Protestant, 171
Proverbs, Book of, 11, 113, 120—
    121, 128, 129
Psalms, Book of, 11, 19, 29, 113,
    116—117, 118, 121, 292
punishment, 62—63

Q

quail, 28
Quirinius, 214
Qumrum, 192

R

Rachel, 35, 129, 214
Rahab, 68, 71
rainbow, 27
Ramoth-Gilead, Battle of, 153
Raphael, Archangel, 173
raven, 26, 28
Rebecca, 34—35
Red Sea
  parting of, 39
reed pipe, 119
Rehoboam, 72, 91, 95
Resurrection, 231, 232, 244, 251,
    252, 266, 282
Reuben (son of Jacob), 72
Revelation, Book of, 10, 13, 87, 119,
    143, 288, 306, 308—309,
    311
rhythm bones, 119
ritual fast, 47
Roman Catholic, 171, 208, 268
Roman empire, 87
Roman occupation, 194
Rome, 167, 177, 183, 186, 191,
    223, 230, 249, 253, 255, 257,

259, 262, 280, 283, 290, 291,
    299, 309
rooster, 28, 29, 241
rules of engagement, 153

Ruth, 84, 214
Ruth, Book of, 65, 78—79

S

Sacrament of Holy Eucharist, 237
sacraments, 268—269
Sacred Tent, 49
Sadducees, 183, 190, 235, 248, 310
Salem, 292
Salome, 219, 225
Samaria, 154, 185, 230, 253, 259
Samaritan, 73
Samson, 75, 77, 266
Samuel, 80, 82, 84, 89, 94, 214
Samuel, First Book of, 65, 80—87
Samuel, Second Book of, 65, 80—87
Sanhedrin, 183, 241, 274
Sarah, 173, 293
Sarai, 30, 32—33. *See also* Sarah
Satan, 115, 239, 305
Saul, King, 65, 80, 82, 83, 84—85,
    118
scriptures, 19
Sea of Galilee, 231
Second Coming, 288, 300, 301, 308
Seleucid, 177
Sermon on the Mount, 227, 295
sermons, 226
seven trumpets, 119
sexuality, 128—129
Shavuot, 149
Sheba, Queen of, 54, 90
Shem, 30, 31
Shema, 60
shepherd, 84
Shiloh, 80, 82
shofar, 119

CREDITS

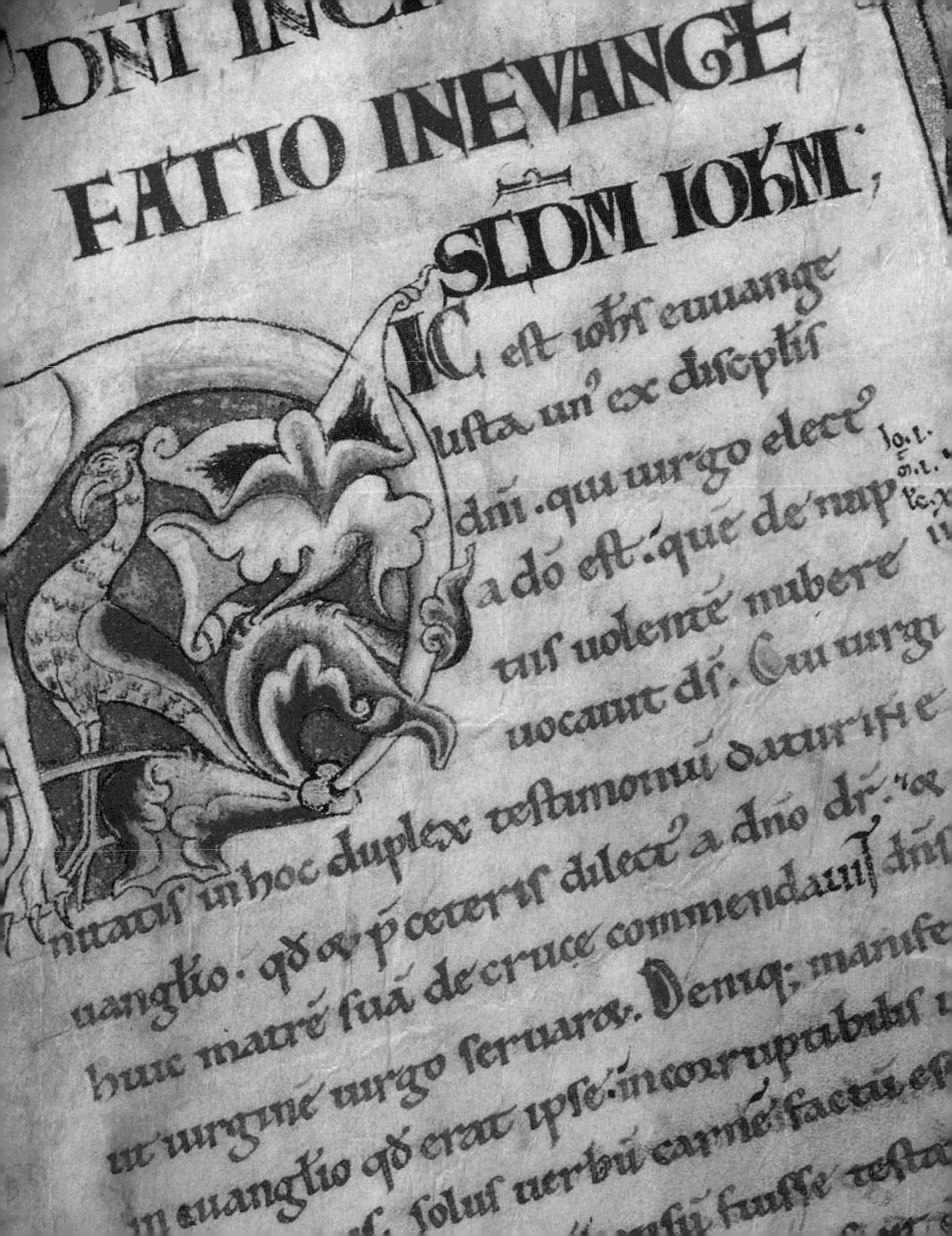

DNI INCI
FATIO INEVANGE
SCDM IOHM
IC est iohs euuange
lista un' ex disciplis
dni. qui uirgo elect'
a do est. que de nup
tiis uolente nubere
uocauit ds. Cui uirgi
nitatis in hoc duplex testimoniu datur in e
uangelio. qd et p ceteris dilect' a dno dr. et
huic matre sua de cruce commendauit dns
ut uirgine uirgo seruaret. Deniq: manife
in euangelio qd erat ipse incorruptibilis u
solus uerbu carne factu e
nsu fuisse testa